"*Confronting Sacred Inequalities* is as sobering as it is hopeful. Leanne Dzubinski paints a well-researched and heartbreaking picture of what women experience every day in the workplace. Her analysis demands our full attention. She lays out a clear biblical rationale, along with practical strategies for how we can improve. Early in each chapter, I mourned the reality that Dzubinski reveals, and by the end of each chapter, I felt more convinced that we can bring about change. It's a rare quality to confront and provide hope. Dzubinski masterfully accomplishes both. *Confronting Sacred Inequalities* is an essential read for all people, and especially my fellow male leaders."

—**Gregg Okesson**, Asbury Theological Seminary

"From stained-glass divisions to cultural stereotypes, *Confronting Sacred Inequalities* is an exceptional guide in navigating workplace expectations for women and men. Thoroughly researched and elegantly written, we have needed this wisdom for years!"

—**Mimi Haddad**, president, CBE International

"Does the church value women the way God does? *Confronting Sacred Inequalities* raises this and other important questions, while compelling Christian organizations to do better than their secular counterparts. Why? Dzubinski says it's because we, as Christians, have both a reason and the resources to do so. Educating us on such terms as 'sanctified sexism' and 'gender-washing,' Dzubinski calls us to create more humane work environments for women and men, while giving us practical suggestions, in gracious and concrete ways, for how to do so. This book is a must-read for leaders who want to foster a more empowering and equitable workplace."

—**Kimberly Battle-Walters Denu**, Westmont College

"Deeply embedded attitudes and practices in many Christian organizations hinder the contributions that women are capable of making. Each of the five gender-related issues addressed by Dzubinski in this book is framed within a context of a helpful synthesis of the relevant literature along with practical suggestions for making Christian organizations healthier workplaces for all. Leaders in Christian organizations will likely find fresh insights and have aha moments that can contribute to more effective leadership."

—**Karen A. Longman**, Azusa Pacific University (emerita)

"It's impossible to fix what you can't see. This is why the church needs a book like *Confronting Sacred Inequalities*, if we are to become a place where women can thrive alongside men in full kingdom service. In this research-based book, Dr. Leanne Dzubinski prophetically exposits five different narratives that plague the church and relegate women to the margins. Read this book if you're serious about helping women to thrive in the church."

—**Rob Dixon**, senior fellow, InterVarsity Institute

Confronting
Sacred
Inequalities

Confronting Sacred Inequalities

CREATING CHRISTIAN ORGANIZATIONS
WHERE WOMEN THRIVE

Leanne M. Dzubinski

B
Baker Academic
a division of Baker Publishing Group
Grand Rapids, Michigan

Published by Baker Academic
a division of Baker Publishing Group
Grand Rapids, Michigan
BakerAcademic.com

Printed in the United States of America

Library of Congress Cataloging-in-Publication Data
Names: Dzubinski, Leanne M., 1963– author
Title: Confronting sacred inequalities : creating Christian organizations where women thrive / Leanne M. Dzubinski.
Description: Grand Rapids, Michigan : Baker Academic, a division of Baker Publishing Group, [2026] | Includes bibliographical references and index.
Identifiers: LCCN 2025022398 | ISBN 9781540967589 paperback | ISBN 9781540969996 casebound | ISBN 9781493453221 ebook | ISBN 9781493453238 pdf
Subjects: LCSH: Women in church work | Misogyny—Religious aspects—Christianity | Sex role—Religious aspects—Christianity | Equality—Religious aspects—Christianity | Christian leadership
Classification: LCC BV4415 .D98 2026
LC record available at https://lccn.loc.gov/2025022398

Portions of this book record the author's present recollection of past events. Dialogue of previous conversations has been re-created and represents the author's accounting of the circumstances in view and not the exact wording of the exchange.

Cover design by Kathleen Lynch / Black Kat Design

Baker Publishing Group publications use paper produced from sustainable forestry practices and postconsumer waste whenever possible.

26   27   28   29   30   31   32   7   6   5   4   3   2   1

Hagar thought, "Have I really seen God and lived to tell about it?" So from then on she called him, "The God Who Sees Me."

Genesis 16:13 CEV

To all the women
who have shared your stories
with me over the years.
You are seen and known.

Contents

Preface

The genesis of this book goes back to 2014. I was one year out from finishing my PhD and had just completed my first year as a professor. My dissertation chair emailed me to let me know of a new conference being held for the first time that year, a conference focused on women in leadership. Because of my dissertation research, she thought I might want to attend. And she was right. I did want to attend. At that conference I met Dr. Amy Diehl. Amy was also just one year out from completing her PhD. As we got to know each other and started talking, we discovered we had done similar research with very different groups of women. I had studied women leading at the executive level in evangelical mission agencies.[1] She had studied women presidents, provosts, and vice presidents in higher education. Given the very different fields, we thought our participants would have very different experiences. But, wow, were we wrong! The more Amy and I talked, the more we realized that our participants actually had very similar

1. My dissertation was later published. See Leanne M. Dzubinski, *Playing by the Rules: How Women Lead in Evangelical Mission Organizations*, American Society of Missiology Monograph Series 52 (Pickwick, 2021).

experiences. Amy had identified fourteen barriers her women ran into when they tried to lead. We looked at my participants, and we found they had also encountered all fourteen of those barriers. My study had identified twelve other barriers, different from the ones Amy had identified. When we looked at Amy's participants, sure enough, they had experienced all twelve of those barriers in addition to the fourteen Amy had already found. It was only when we had names for the challenges and knew to look for them that we could see them. We put our studies together, and our first publication was called "Making the Invisible Visible"[2]—because that is literally what we did. By understanding what to look for, we were able to see it and name it. And once we can see and name something, then we can deal with it. But if we cannot see it or do not know it is there, we cannot do anything about it.

Amy and I have continued to work together for over a decade now. Together with two other researchers we created a scale to measure women's experiences of bias at work.[3] We have studied the experiences of women in health care, in law, in higher education, and in mission agencies. We have looked at public accounts of women's experiences from just about every conceivable field. And what we have learned is that no matter the industry or field, women bump up against the same barriers. We call them "Glass Walls," and we explain and illustrate them in our book called *Glass Walls: Shattering the Six Gender Bias Barriers Still Holding Women Back at Work*.[4]

2. Amy B. Diehl and Leanne M. Dzubinski, "Making the Invisible Visible: A Cross-Sector Analysis of Gender-Based Leadership Barriers," *Human Resource Development Quarterly* 27, no. 2 (2016): 181–206.

3. Amy B. Diehl et al., "Measuring the Invisible: Development and Multi-Industry Validation of the Gender Bias Scale for Women Leaders," *Human Resource Development Quarterly* 31, no. 3 (2020): 249–80.

4. Amy B. Diehl and Leanne M. Dzubinski, *Glass Walls: Shattering the Six Gender Bias Barriers That Still Hold Women Back at Work* (Rowman & Littlefield, 2023).

But these barriers are not limited to present-day women or to US or Western women. In my work with Dr. Anneke Stasson of Indiana Wesleyan University, we wanted to understand women's contributions to the growth of the church and the spread of Christianity from New Testament times to the present. We discovered several important things. First, women have truly been instrumental in the growth of the church and the spread of the gospel. Their stories have just gotten less attention than men's stories, a trend that historians today are working to change. Second, in every time period women encountered obstacles to their leadership from both society and the church. And in every time period women learned how to turn those constraints into assets. In so doing they contributed to the theology of the church and were faithful even to the point of death. In following Jesus's call they also challenged their own culture's notions of womanhood. In every time and culture, society writes scripts for women, and those scripts are not necessarily designed for women to flourish. Christian women throughout history have been willing to challenge those scripts for the good of themselves and also for the growth of the church. Our book *Women in the Mission of the Church* tells the stories of many of these faithful women.[5]

This book pulls together threads from each of my previous works. The focus of this book is women in present-day Christian organizations, be they churches, universities, seminaries, mission agencies, nonprofits, or any other type of faith-based organization. The topic is gendered attitudes and practices prevalent in Christian organizations that make it hard for women to flourish. These challenges also make it difficult for women and men to work collegially together, and, in the end, hinder the organization from effectively achieving its goals.

5. Leanne M. Dzubinski and Anneke H. Stasson, *Women in the Mission of the Church: Their Opportunities and Obstacles Throughout Christian History* (Baker Academic, 2021).

Experience tells me that the primary readers of this book will be women. After all, it is a man's world and women are the ones who do the work to understand and play the game by men's rules. Nevertheless, my hope and prayer is that men will also read this book. Men who love God, who love their sisters in Christ, and who want to see the people in their organizations flourish. Men like my editor, Jim Kinney, who asked for this book because he is already doing the work. Men like my husband, Paul Dzubinski, who is a champion for women in his organization. Many men I have worked with over the years care deeply about these issues. May this book expand your understanding and give you tools and strategies to continue making the world a better place.

Introduction

Women hold up half the sky.

—Mao Zedong

"Women hold up half the sky" is a statement made by the Chinese Communist Party chairman Mao Zedong in 1949.[1] The phrase has been picked up by others, including Nicholas Kristof and Sheryl WuDunn in their 2009 book *Half the Sky: Turning Oppression into Opportunity for Women Worldwide* and Carolyn Custis James in her 2011 book *Half the Church: Recapturing God's Global Vision for Women.* I do not know what Mao thought when he made that statement, but I do know that God had planned something similar for humanity at the dawn of time. The Genesis origin story tells how male and female came to be, and how God instructed male and female to work together in the garden he had made for them. God's original intent was indeed for women to hold up half the sky, yet human history has deviated very far from

---

1. Valarie Tan, "Women Hold Up Half the Sky, but Men Rule the Party," Mercator Institute for China Studies, July 3, 2021, https://merics.org/en/comment /women-hold-half-sky-men-rule-party.

that ideal. What would it take to get back on track? Specifically, what would it take for Christian organizations to restore the healthy interactions between women and men that God intended from the beginning?

I have been studying women's experiences in Christian organizations for twenty years now. One of the common statements I hear from Christian women, after they describe their experiences to me, is that Christian organizations are "thirty years behind" the rest of the world in how they treat women. I used to believe that was true, thinking women in secular organizations had more legal protections and better experiences than my friends and I in mission agencies and Christian universities. Time and further research have proven me wrong. No matter what time period I study, or what industry I examine, women experience challenges at work that their male colleagues simply do not encounter. After two decades of study, my conclusion is that the problem does not lie with any particular field or industry or type of work; the problem is that women are working while female.

What I have learned through my research is both good news and bad news for Christian organizations. The good news is that Christian organizations are not thirty years behind. Christian organizations are similar to every other type of organization in the US. But the bad news is that Christian organizations are not any better than our secular counterparts. Yet they should be. Christians have both the reasons and the resources to do better. Christians are called one body in Christ (1 Cor. 12:12–27). Christians understand the gifts of the spirit (Rom. 12:4–8; 1 Cor. 12:7–11, 28–31). Christians have the knowledge of being joint heirs with Christ (Rom. 8:17).

And Christians are called siblings—brothers and sisters—in Christ's body, the church. Romans 12:1–3 explains:

I appeal to you therefore, brothers and sisters, on the basis of God's mercy, to present your bodies as a living sacrifice, holy and acceptable to God, which is your reasonable act of worship. Do not be conformed to this age, but be transformed by the renewing of the mind, so that you may discern what is the will of God—what is good and acceptable and perfect. For by the grace given to me I say to everyone among you not to think of yourself more highly than you ought to think but to think with sober judgment, each according to the measure of faith that God has assigned.[2]

As siblings in Christ, Christians are not to think more highly of some over others, as James 2:1–9 also states, warning against discrimination among believers.

Rather, Christians are fellow priests in God's kingdom, as 1 Peter 2:9 says: "But you are a chosen people, a royal priesthood, a holy nation, God's own people, in order that you may proclaim the excellence of him who called you out of darkness into his marvelous light." Christians are not chosen by God, priests, and holy people belonging to God just for our own benefit. Christians have a specific purpose: to make God's excellence known to the world.

Because of the reasons and resources Christians have as the body of Christ, followers of Christ should be doing better than anyone else at treating each other well, creating healthy work environments where everyone can thrive, and showing the world how women and men can live in partnership and harmony. But that is too often not the case. Sometimes Christians even lag behind. A number of recent books have sought to call attention to the challenges Christians and Christian organizations face regarding women's participation in ministry and leadership. Beth Moore,[3] Beth Allison Barr,[4] Kristin Kobes Du Mez,[5] and the

---

2. Unless otherwise indicated, I have used the NRSVue for Scripture quotations.

3. Beth Moore, *All My Knotted-Up Life: A Memoir* (Tyndale, 2023).

4. Beth Allison Barr, *The Making of Biblical Womanhood: How the Subjugation of Women Became Gospel Truth* (Brazos, 2021).

5. Kristin Kobes Du Mez, *Jesus and John Wayne: How White Evangelicals Corrupted a Faith and Fractured a Nation* (Liveright, 2020).

report on the Southern Baptist Convention's abuse allegations[6] are just a few publications in recent times calling out unhealthy Christian systems. While such reports are an important and necessary step in diagnosing the problem, helping to name and make visible the challenges women face, more is needed. Steps toward health and strategies for wholeness are also needed. A better Christian response for a broken, hurting world is needed. That is what this book is about.

Important Notes

Before I give an overview of each chapter, I want to note and acknowledge a couple of important points about this book. The first point is about sex and gender. This book is mostly written from the perspective of a gender binary, because that is the area where I have done research. The bulk of my data comes from those who identify as female. I have not done research with men or with gender nonconforming people. Of course, there are many other kinds of marginalization that happen in Christian organizations based on identity factors such as gender, race, ethnicity, age, and so many more.[7] Much more work is needed in these other areas as well, and I hope others will continue to press into those important questions. My task in this book is to focus primarily on issues that arise for those who identify as female.

6. *The Southern Baptist Convention Executive Committee's Response to Sexual Abuse Allegations and an Audit of the Procedures and Actions of the Credentials Committee* (Guidepost Solutions, May 15, 2022), available at https://www.documentcloud.org/documents/22028383-guidepost-investigation-of-the-southern-baptist-convention/.
7. Amy B. Diehl, Leanne M. Dzubinski, and Amber L. Stephenson, "How Organizations Can Recognize—and End—Gendered Ageism," in *Overcoming Ageism*, Women at Work Series (Harvard Business Review Press, 2024), 171–78; Amy B. Diehl, Leanne M. Dzubinski, and Amber L. Stephenson, "Never Quite Right: Identity Factors Contributing to Bias and Discrimination Experienced by Women Leaders in the United States," *Human Resource Development Quarterly* (2024): 1–20.

The second note is about issues of intersectionality related to race and ethnicity. Abundant research shows that whatever challenges white women face, women of color face as well, though sometimes in a different format and often in an intensified way. For example, chapter 1 presents the issue of the sexualization of women. This problem is ubiquitous across time and cultures and is performed relative to the different cultural stereotypes of women that prevail in that time and space. Similarly, disbelieving women and devaluing them through, for example, unequal pay, is also ubiquitous across time and cultures. And again, the excuses given for such treatment are based on the prevailing cultural stereotypes of any given time and space. In this book I have not attempted to delineate the detailed, specific impact of intersectional factors for every problem presented. Rather, I have sought to address the fundamental issues from which these challenges stem. The work of addressing the specific form of any given problem lies with the leaders of that organization. White men in particular need to work to understand not just gender issues but all the additional intersectional issues that hamper the women in their organization.

Chapter Overview

In this book I name and describe five challenges identified through research that confront Christian organizations today. After describing each challenge, I look at what the Bible says about it. Then I discuss solutions, practical and God-honoring ways to create culture change for the good of women, and therefore for the good of men and organizations as well.

The first chapter, "Sex and the Office," presents the concept of the stained-glass partition that keeps men and women separated at work in an attempt to reduce temptation and misperceptions. This stained-glass partition is based on a sexualized view of women as temptresses. It is devaluing to both men and women; a healthy culture is one where women and men learn to see and treat each other as brothers and sisters in the body of Christ.

The second chapter is titled "Hey, Guys!" and focuses on language that hinders women's flourishing. In it I cover two issues: language that excludes women, and ways of speaking that marginalize women. First, many Christian organizations still default to male-normative language. However, when language is normed to the male experience, women spend time and energy translating the message to discern if and where they fit in. Second, language dynamics in meetings can make it challenging for women to engage. Understanding and correcting language issues can enable organizations to invite women in and to hear the best ideas from both men and women, leading to more productive meetings and better organizational outcomes.

Chapter 3, "I Can't. I Have to Work," introduces five assumptions around how work gets done that create additional challenges for women. All five operate together and reinforce one another in a kind of toxic soup. I start with the concepts of "ideal worker" and "greedy institutions." The ideal worker concept underlies how many organizations have been built, assuming a male breadwinner and a full-time, supportive, stay-at-home wife. The greedy institutions concept explains that many organizations demand workers be available for long, unpredictable hours and be free from outside responsibilities. Then comes the belief in separate spheres, meaning men belong in public and women at home, a Victorian ideal which is further reinforced through gender essentialist beliefs. Last is the two-person career structure, where a man is assumed to have someone taking care of all personal and relational needs while also contributing to his career—which feeds back into and reinforces the ideal worker myth. None of this thinking supports healthy individuals, families, or holistic human flourishing. The COVID-19 pandemic brought disruptive change to how work is done, with new ideas about remote work, flexibility, and hybrid working arrangements. Many of those changes are beneficial for men and women alike. Organizations can examine how they view workers and how work gets done, revising systems and practices to create conditions where all can thrive.

Chapter 4, titled "Are You Sure That's Right?" presents the various ways ambivalence toward women crops up at work. From language that portrays women as less important than men, to disbelief of women's statements, to lack of support and inadequate pay, to benevolent and sanctified sexism, all these forms of ambivalence hamper women at work. The chapter lays out concrete strategies for leaders to treat women in the workplace as full, equal partners.

The last chapter, chapter 5, is called "There Are No Good Women Leaders." It unpacks social gender role stereotypes, which explain why women are not typically associated with leadership qualities. Then it considers evangelical gender role prescriptions for women, showing how they are in reality just social role stereotypes in Christian language. Then the negative consequences of holding to such stereotypes are unpacked. Solutions for the negative consequences as well as ways to counter stereotypical thinking are presented. Seeing people as whole humans, not roles and stereotypes, helps women and men thrive and yields better organizational outcomes.

Who Should Read This Book?

If you are a woman in a Christian workplace, I hope you will find this book informative and validating. One of the common responses I hear from women after I talk about these issues is something along the lines of "Oh! It's not just me!" And indeed it is not. These challenges are common to women in virtually all workplaces and can be especially present for women in Christian organizations.

I also hope men working in Christian organizations will read this book. It will help you understand women in your organization. It may help you empathize with some of their challenges and enable you to see organizational practices and structures in a different light. It will help you be a better ally for women and perhaps even help you advocate for changes that could be beneficial to everyone.

Finally, and most importantly, I hope male organizational leaders will read this book and take its message to heart. You are the ones with power and authority to make change. You are the ones who can make resources available to create healthier working environments for everyone. It is time to step up and create Christian organizations that are truly different from—and better than—any other workplaces.

1

"Sex and the Office"

The Problem with a Stained-Glass Partition

> It's never fun to experience the Billy Graham rule. And I've had that experience before. I showed up to ride with [my colleague] . . . to meet this donor, and his wife was in the car with him. His wife didn't know the donor, so why is she here?
>
> —female professor[1]

Many Christians are familiar with the Billy Graham rule. According to his autobiography, back in the 1940s Dr. Graham worked with a band of evangelists, traveling and sharing the gospel.[2] These men were deeply concerned

1. Leanne M. Dzubinski, M. Elizabeth Lewis Hall, and Richard L. Starcher, "The Stained-Glass Partition: Cross-Sex Collegial Relationships in Christian Academia," *Christian Higher Education* 20, no. 3 (2020): 191.
2. "What's 'the Billy Graham Rule'?," Billy Graham Evangelistic Association, July 23, 2019, https://billygraham.org/story/the-modesto-manifesto-a-declaration

with the integrity of their ministry and wanted to avoid problems they had seen happen with other evangelists. So they came
to consensus on four big issues: financial integrity, sexual moral-
ity, publicity, and church partnerships. One of them, the worry
about sexual impropriety, has garnered a lot of attention. Here
is their agreement: "We pledged among ourselves to avoid any
situation that would have even the appearance of compromise
or suspicion. From that day on, I did not travel, meet or eat
alone with a woman other than my wife."[3] This rule became
popular and has been picked up and perpetuated among male
ministry leaders, and many other men, right up to the present day. It received renewed interest a few years ago when *The
Washington Post* reported that then Vice President Mike Pence
would not eat "alone with a woman other than his wife."[4] The
Post article rekindled discussion and debate about the "rule"
keeping men and women separate, and the varied consequences
that it could have for men, women, and families.

Proponents of the rule point to the destruction that can
happen in a marriage when a spouse is unfaithful. They focus
on the sanctity of marriage and the importance of healthy,
trusting relationships between husbands and wives. Yet the rule
also has downsides. Most top-level leadership in the United
States is still male dominated, so preventing men from meeting with or mentoring junior women can negatively impact
women's career progress. And some question the effectiveness
of the rule: If people want to do something, they can usually
find a way.

-of-biblical-integrity/. The other three members of the team were Cliff Barrows,
George Beverly Shea, and Grady Wilson.

    3. "What's 'the Billy Graham Rule'?"

    4. "Karen Pence Is the Vice President's 'Prayer Warrior,'" *Washington Post*,
March 28, 2017, https://www.washingtonpost.com/politics/karen-pence-is-the
-vice-presidents-prayer-warrior-gut-check-and-shield/2017/03/28/3d7a26ce-0a01
-11e7-8884-96e6a6713f4b_story.html.

The Glass Partition

Since men are employed at higher rates than women[5] and since men are thought to be more subject to sexual temptation than women,[6] many workplaces default to a structure that helps men feel more comfortable by keeping them relatively segregated from women at work. This segregation happens in secular organizations as well as in Christian ones. Kim Elsesser and Letitia Peplau identified this tendency in 2006 and named it the "glass partition."[7] Their research with forty-one working professionals, twenty-one women and twenty men, showed that employees worried about perceptions: Would their work friend or other colleagues mistake friendship for romantic interest? And they worried about friendly comments or jokes being mistaken for sexual harassment.

Later, Elsesser further developed her research into a book provocatively titled *Sex and the Office: Women, Men, and the Sex Partition That's Dividing the Workforce.*[8] She describes the partition this way: "In order to avoid any suggestion of workplace romance or sexual harassment, opposite-sex coworkers are shying away from nonessential interactions, creating a barrier between men and women at work. Friendships with the

5. According to the U.S. Bureau for Labor Statistics, in 2022 67.9 percent of men over the age of twenty-five were employed, compared with 55.4 percent of women. Men also have higher employment ratios than women for all educational levels. "Employment Differences of Men and Women Narrow with Educational Attainment," Bureau of Labor Statistics, July 28, 2023, https://www.bls.gov/opub /ted/2023/employment-differences-of-men-and-women-narrow-with-educational -attainment.htm.

6. See, for example, Stephen Arterburn and Fred Stoeker, *Every Man's Battle: Winning the War on Sexual Temptation One Victory at a Time*, 20th anniv. ed. (WaterBrook, 2020); Brendan Jamal Thornton, "Victims of Illicit Desire: Pentecostal Men of God and the Specter of Sexual Temptation," *Anthropological Quarterly* 91, no. 1 (2018): 133–71.

7. Kim Elsesser and Letitia Anne Peplau, "The Glass Partition: Obstacles to Cross-Sex Friendships at Work," *Human Relations* 59, no. 8 (2006): 1077–1100.

8. Kim Elsesser, *Sex and the Office: Women, Men, and the Sex Partition That's Dividing the Workplace* (Taylor Trade Publishing, 2015).

opposite sex can be tricky enough to manage outside of work, but within the workplace, additional constraints encourage workers to stick to same-sex colleagues. These barriers between the sexes that get in the way of developing cross-sex friendships make up what I call the *sex partition*."[9]

Notice the two reasons she cites for creating the partition: worries about romance (real or perceived) and worries about sexual harassment (again, actual or perceived). Those worries come from both sides. If a colleague suggests discussing a workplace matter over lunch with a colleague of the opposite sex, both parties may wonder: Is the other person thinking of it as a date? Are they interested in me? If I accept, will they think I'm interested in them? The possibilities for questioning are endless and may make people feel insecure and unable to read the signs. The same perception problems can happen around harassment (though harassment is more commonly directed from men toward women):[10] A man can worry that his statement will be misperceived as harassment or that a female colleague will misunderstand his intentions. The line between friendliness and harassment may appear to be fuzzy, especially in workplaces that don't offer good training on the topic.[11] So, in the end, for everyone, the simplest solution may appear to be the partition.

Elsesser points out one of the big problems with the sex partition at work, though: It limits people's abilities to build workplace friendships. And the lack of friendships at work

---

9. Elsesser, *Sex and the Office*, 4 (italics in original).

10. Fredrik Bondestam and Maja Lundqvist, "Sexual Harassment in Higher Education—a Systematic Review," *European Journal of Higher Education* 10, no. 4 (2020): 397–98.

11. Bondestam and Lundqvist, "Sexual Harassment," 407. The authors commented that "men who *do not* participate in training on what constitutes sexual harassment are less inclined to see or define sexually harassing behaviors as in fact sexual harassment" (407, italics in original). Training is crucial to help employees know what is and is not harassment.

can be costly: "The sex partition limits your pool of potential friends, and limiting your friends also limits your career. The benefits of friendships at work extend far beyond having buddies at the water cooler. Friends at work provide one another with valuable information, and [friendships] with more senior employees can evolve into mentor relationships. The research evidence is irrefutable: Those with more work friends earn more money, get promoted faster, have better job performance, are happier in their jobs, and have better health than those with fewer friends."[12] That is a long list of good reasons why workplace friendships matter. What organization and what employee would not want those outcomes?

For women, friendships with male colleagues at work may be particularly important. Men still hold the majority of leadership roles.[13] Men still control the majority of organizational resources. As new employees, men typically learn the culture, expectations, and resources of an organization more quickly—precisely because they have easier access to friendships, networks, and information—than women do. Women's lack of access to such resources can become a significant hindrance to completing their jobs and to progressing in their careers.

Recently I was invited to speak at an out-of-state venue. The organizer promised to cover my costs and asked me to make my own travel plans. Right before the trip, I received an email asking me to cancel my hotel reservation because she had learned that her university had an account at a local hotel. When I arrived, she explained that she had been working there for over ten years and never knew about the university account. So for ten years she had been paying out of her own budget while her

---

12. Elsesser, *Sex and the Office*, 4.
13. Catalyst reports that in 2022 women made up only 8.8 percent of Fortune 500 CEO roles. And in 2021 they held only 30 percent of S&P 500 board memberships. Catalyst, *Women in the Workforce: United States* (2022), https://www.catalyst.org/insights/2022/women-in-the-workforce-united-states.

male colleagues were having their speaker costs subsidized by the university. She was understandably frustrated!

Consider the potential consequences: Lacking knowledge of organizational resources meant she was able to bring fewer guest speakers within her budget, which in turn could potentially impact her perceived contribution to the university, impact her student evaluations compared to male peers, and even hinder her promotion. All because she lacked access to information that a work friend could have shared with her.

The Stained-Glass Partition

When the glass partition is at work in a Christian organization, it is known as the stained-glass partition or "gender separation in a Christian . . . atmosphere."[14] The stained-glass partition may be constructed intentionally through policies and practices (such as the Pence/Graham rule) that set boundaries around when and how men and women may interact with one another. Or it may arise passively, because it seems convenient or because women seem invisible to their male colleagues.[15] Both men and women may intentionally erect a personal stained-glass partition, though their reasons typically differ. Men may preemptively construct a stained-glass partition through fear of being misperceived or tempted. Women, on the other hand, may responsively construct the partition based on real harm they have experienced in the past.[16]

Regardless of the reasons, the partition often has specific, gendered impact on women. In Christian colleges and universities, for example, female students typically comprise about two-thirds of the student body, but women faculty hover

---

14. Dzubinski, Hall, and Starcher, "Stained-Glass Partition," 189.
15. Dzubinski, Hall, and Starcher, "Stained-Glass Partition," 190–94.
16. Dzubinski, Hall, and Starcher, "Stained-Glass Partition," 192–93.

between 33–45 percent.[17] In such settings, women report higher workloads in student advising, especially if, as sometimes happens, male faculty refuse to mentor or advise female students.[18] Women may also be expected to serve on more committees, under the guise of including a female voice, yet without considering the overall additional workload. The phenomenon of some people bearing extra load in the university is called "identity taxation," meaning a faculty member who belongs to a "historically marginalized group within their department or university" is expected to perform additional work beyond what is normally expected of other faculty members.[19] For women, those expectations may include mentoring female students and performing additional teaching and service compared to male colleagues.[20] Next, women may personalize these struggles, thinking the problem lies within themselves, since they do not see their male colleagues having the same challenges.[21] One effect for faculty is that women progress more slowly in their research and in their careers than their male colleagues.[22] Another result is that more women leave the institution than do men.[23]

It is easy to see how similar dynamics can exist in churches, mission agencies, and other Christian organizations. In my

17. Jeff Clawson et al., *2021 Report on Diversity at CCCU Institutions* (SCIO, 2021), https://www.scio-uk.org/wp-content/uploads/2021/09/2021-Report-on-Diversity-at-CCCU-Institutions.pdf; Karen A. Longman and Patricia S. Anderson, "Women in Leadership: The Future of Christian Higher Education," *Christian Higher Education* 15, nos. 1–2 (2016): 24.

18. Dzubinski, Hall, and Starcher, "Stained-Glass Partition," 191.

19. Laura E. Hirschfield and Tiffany D. Joseph, "'We Need a Woman, We Need a Black Woman': Gender, Race, and Identity Taxation in the Academy," *Gender and Education* 24, no. 2 (2012): 214.

20. Hirschfield and Joseph, "'We Need a Woman,'" 213.

21. Personalizing happens when women assume "personal responsibility for system or organizational problems" beyond their control. Amy B. Diehl and Leanne M. Dzubinski, "Making the Invisible Visible: A Cross-Sector Analysis of Gender-Based Leadership Barriers," *Human Resource Development Quarterly* 27, no. 2 (2016): 192.

22. Hirschfield and Joseph, "'We Need a Woman,'" 214.

23. Dzubinski, Hall, and Starcher, "Stained-Glass Partition," 194–95.

study of mission agencies, I heard several stories of men who refused to work with or report to women.[24] In some cases, the Pence/Graham rule is carried out so strenuously that it amounts to men shunning their women colleagues by flat-out refusing to work with or even speak to them.[25] When it comes to mentoring, organizational dynamics can be remarkably similar to the faculty/student relationship. Most organizations, Christian and secular, remain heavily male dominated at the higher ranks.[26] But they may be more gender balanced at the lower ranks.[27] Thus high-ranking male leaders who refuse to mentor or develop junior women create two problems for the organization. First is the lack of development for junior women, and second is the additional burden placed on any upper-level women in the organization to take on additional work mentoring junior colleagues.

The combined effects of the stained-glass partition can be substantial. Friendships at work are important for emotional health and work productivity. Limiting women's access to men, and especially higher-ranking men, can impede their career progress, limiting their ability to grow and progress professionally. Organizations may place travel limits on men and women, requiring completely separate transportation to professional development events or work conferences, but then not provide

24. Leanne M. Dzubinski, *Playing by the Rules: How Women Lead in Evangelical Mission Organizations*, American Society of Missiology Monograph Series 52 (Pickwick, 2021), 174–77, 81.

25. Amy B. Diehl and Leanne M. Dzubinski, *Glass Walls: Shattering the Six Gender Bias Barriers That Still Hold Women Back at Work* (Rowman & Littlefield, 2023), 21.

26. Catalyst, *Women in the Workforce*; Liz Elting, "More Women Lead Top Companies Than Ever, and It's Not Even Close to Enough," *Forbes*, June 15, 2024, https://www.forbes.com/sites/lizelting/2024/06/15/more-women-lead-top-companies-than-ever-and-its-not-even-close-to-enough/; Amy Reynolds, Janel Curry, and Neil Carlson, *Gender Dynamics in Evangelical Institutions: Women and Men Leading in Higher Education and the Non-Profit Sector*, Women in Leadership National Study (Gordon College, 2016), 5–6.

27. Catalyst, *Women in the Workforce*.

sufficient funding for both men and women to attend. Sometimes these travel decisions fail to take into account women's safety and security needs, leaving women to take public transit or local transportation alone in late or unsafe circumstances in order to preserve the appearance that male and female colleagues are traveling separately. Thus in virtually every way, women are typically the ones disadvantaged: They may miss the opportunity, be expected to fund their own way rather than being covered by the organizational budget, and be left on their own to handle unsafe situations.

The emotional impact for women can also be devastating. They feel distrusted and, worse, unable to protest. When men use the Pence/Graham rule to justify not carrying their share of the load or not supporting their women colleagues, they have effectively used a form of "sanctified sexism" to excuse their behavior.[28] The power of religion produces "an implied finality or non-negotiability about the discriminatory behavior."[29] When Christian men use the Pence/Graham rule as a reason to fail to support, mentor, and develop their female colleagues, or to place additional burden on them in terms of workload or travel, women may feel that pushing back is impossible because it would seem like arguing with God.

Nevertheless, Christian institutions desire to maintain high standards of sexual purity and to value marriage, family, and singleness alike. Those are worthwhile goals in a fractured and broken world. So how can organizations think in healthy Christian ways about male-female interactions in the workplace?

---

28. M. Elizabeth Lewis Hall, Brad Christerson, and Shelly Cunningham, "Sanctified Sexism: Religious Beliefs and the Gender Harassment of Academic Women," *Psychology of Women Quarterly* 34, no. 2 (2010): 181. They describe sanctified sexism as schemas based on religion that are used to justify sexist treatment of women (182). See chap. 4 for more on sanctified sexism.

29. Hall, Christerson, and Cunningham, "Sanctified Sexism," 182.

Scripture's Perspective

In this section I look at what the Bible has to say about men and women who follow Jesus: It portrays them as siblings. Scot McKnight explains that "siblingship" is the primary understanding of relationships in the church.[30] He adds, "Nurturing a local church in which each person is a brother or sister is the heart of pastoral ministry for Paul."[31] While McKnight's main point is to contrast family relationships with friendship relationships, the understanding that Christians are family— siblings—in the body of Christ helps Christians move beyond seeing one another primarily as potential sexual partners. A sibling relationship is not a sexual relationship!

When thinking about what the New Testament says about siblings, a little Greek study is helpful. The terms *adelphos* (masculine singular, often translated as "brother") and *adelphoi* (masculine plural, often translated as "brothers") are inclusive terms. *Adelphos* can simply mean a fellow believer, without specifying male gender. Similarly, *adelphoi* can mean "believers" and includes both men and women.[32] In both cases the terms are functioning metaphorically, since the relationship is not one of literal blood kinship. The frequency of the sibling metaphor—271 uses in the New Testament—indicates that "the idea of siblingship is the dominant self-understanding and self-designation of the church."[33]

Unfortunately, not all Bible translations make the sibling relationship clear to modern readers. English today does not use the masculine singular and plural as inclusive or not

30. Scot McKnight, *Pastor Paul: Nurturing a Culture of Christoformity in the Church*, Theological Explorations for the Church Catholic (Brazos, 2019), 60–61.
31. McKnight, *Pastor Paul*, 60.
32. See McKnight, *Pastor Paul*, 60–61. See also Marg Mowczko, "'Brothers and Sisters' (Adelphoi) in Paul's Letters," *Exploring the Biblical Theology of Christian Egalitarianism* (blog), March 25, 2022, https://margmowczko.com/adelphoi -brothers-and-sisters/#_ftn1.
33. McKnight, *Pastor Paul*, 61.

indicating gender. To the contrary, English readers who see "he" or "brother" understand that language to mean males, not females. Educational institutions and publishing guidelines have specified for decades that masculine terms are only to be used for males.[34] Yet some Bible translations continue to use outdated language that obscures the Bible's actual message. The ESV, for example, translates *adelphoi* as "brothers," and then it footnotes the term with the notation "or brothers and sisters."[35] The NIV is less consistent, but in Matthew 23:8 it translates *adelphoi* as "brothers."[36]

The point of these passages is not gender; the biblical authors are not discussing male-female relationships or anything specific to males and females. Rather, they are discussing how Christians, fellow believers, are to behave and live together in Christian community. Obscuring the presence of women in these discussions makes no sense in terms of church order. It only makes sense as an intentional linguistic strategy to show preference to men and make women invisible in the body of Christ.[37]

34. See, for example, the *Publication Manual of the American Psychological Association*, *The Chicago Manual of Style*, and the Baker Academic style guidelines for examples of such guidance.

35. The preface to the ESV explains, "Similarly, the English word 'brothers' (translating the Greek word *adelphoi*) is retained as an important familial form of address between fellow-Jews and fellow-Christians in the first century. A recurring note is included to indicate that the term 'brothers' (*adelphoi*) was often used in Greek to refer to both men and women, and to indicate the specific instances in the text where this is the case" (see "Preface to the Standard English Version," https://www.esv.org/preface/). See also Marg Mowczko, "Manhood and Masculinity in the ESV," *Exploring the Biblical Theology of Christian Egalitarianism* (blog), August 11, 2019, https://margmowczko.com/biblical-manhood-masculinity-esv/. Language is covered more thoroughly in chap. 2.

36. The verse reads, "But you are not to be called 'Rabbi,' for you have one Teacher, and you are all brothers." The inconsistency can be seen in 1 Cor. 6, where Paul discusses lawsuits among fellow believers. In v. 6 the NIV renders *adelphos* as "brother": "one brother takes another to court." Then in v. 8 it renders *adelphoi* as "brothers and sisters": "Instead, you yourselves cheat and do wrong, and you do this to your brothers and sisters."

37. Mowczko, "Manhood and Masculinity in the ESV." Apparently the translators fully intend to give primacy to men.

The concept of believers being siblings in Christ started with Jesus. In Matthew 23:8, Jesus tells the crowds, "You have one teacher, and you are all brothers and sisters." Mark 3 records an instance when Jesus's biological mother and brothers arrived, and Jesus responded, "'Who are my mother and my brothers?' And looking at those who sat around him, he said, 'Here are my mother and my brothers! Whoever does the will of God is my brother and sister and mother'" (3:33–35). In Mark 10 there is another instance of Jesus calling his followers his brothers and sisters. Peter points out that the disciples have left everything behind in order to follow Jesus.[38] And Jesus's reply is interesting in that it encompasses both literal siblings and metaphorical ones. Jesus replies, "Truly I tell you, there is no one who has left house or brothers or sisters or mother or father or children or fields for my sake and for the sake of the good news who will not receive a hundredfold now in this age—houses, brothers and sisters, mothers and children, and fields, with persecutions—and in the age to come eternal life" (10:29–30). In the first part of his statement, Jesus refers to literal relationships among kinfolk; the second part refers to relationships among his followers, who are now fictive kin, related not by blood or marriage but by agreement in following Jesus.[39] What these stories have in common is Jesus's understanding of how his followers were to relate to one another: as family, as siblings.

Paul picks up on this idea and amplifies it throughout his writings in the New Testament. For example, in a well-known and often-quoted passage, Romans 8:28–30, Paul writes, "And we know that in all things God works for the good of those

38. The disciples were not all men. When the Bible talks about "the twelve," it does mean the twelve disciples Jesus called. But often when speaking of disciples, Scripture means all those who were followers, including women. See, for example, Luke 8:1–3; Acts 1:13–14.

39. Encyclopedia.com, "fictive kinship," accessed November 17, 2023, https://www.encyclopedia.com/reference/encyclopedias-almanacs-transcripts-and-maps/fictive-kinship.

who love him, who have been called according to his purpose. For those God foreknew he also predestined to be conformed to the image of his Son, that he might be the firstborn among many brothers and sisters. And those he predestined, he also called; those he called, he also justified; those he justified, he also glorified" (NIV). Another commonly quoted passage, Romans 12:1–2, also addresses believers as siblings: "I appeal to you therefore, brothers and sisters, on the basis of God's mercy, to present your bodies as a living sacrifice, holy and acceptable to God, which is your reasonable act of worship. Do not be conformed to this age, but be transformed by the renewing of the mind, so that you may discern what is the will of God—what is good and acceptable and perfect." The sibling relationship is therefore a strong metaphor for Christians to follow.[40]

In addition to addressing Christians as brothers and sisters, the New Testament talks about Christians being "adopted" as siblings with Jesus and children of God. Paul explains to the believers in Rome: "For you did not receive a spirit of slavery to fall back into fear, but you received a spirit of adoption. When we cry, 'Abba! Father!' it is that very Spirit bearing witness with our spirit that we are children of God, and if children, then heirs: heirs of God and joint heirs with Christ, if we in fact suffer with him so that we may also be glorified with him" (Rom. 8:15–17). Similarly, Ephesians 1 explains:

> Blessed be the God and Father of our Lord Jesus Christ, who has blessed us in Christ with every spiritual blessing in the heavenly places, just as he chose us in Christ before the foundation of the world to be holy and blameless before him in love. He destined

---

40. I am aware that the sibling relationship is not always positive, and that family metaphors taken too far in Christian organizations can also be problematic, even destructive. See chap. 4 for more on the dark side of overemphasizing organizational members as family.

us for adoption as his children through Jesus Christ, according to the good pleasure of his will. . . . In Christ we have also obtained an inheritance, having been destined according to the purpose of him who accomplishes all things according to his counsel and will, so that we, who were the first to set our hope on Christ, might live for the praise of his glory. (1:3–5, 11–12)

Being adopted by God and having an inheritance in Jesus sets Christians up as siblings in the body of Christ.

Finally, the New Testament offers several commands for fellow believers to love each other as siblings. For example, the writer of Hebrews exhorts readers: "Keep on loving one another as brothers and sisters" (Heb. 13:1 NIV). And John commands fellow believers to love one another as well: "Those who say, 'I love God,' and hate a brother or sister are liars, for those who do not love a brother or sister, whom they have seen, cannot love God, whom they have not seen. The commandment we have from him is this: those who love God must love their brothers and sisters also" (1 John 4:20–21). The consequences of loving one another are also interesting and highly pertinent to the topic of this chapter. "Whoever loves a brother or sister abides in the light, and in such a person there is no cause for stumbling" (2:10).

Not stumbling, or having no "offense" or "scandal," is exactly the worry with which this chapter started and is the concern that leads to a stained-glass partition and a Pence/Graham rule in the workplace. And what prescription does the New Testament offer for not stumbling and not causing offense with one another? Not a wall or a partition or a rule. Rather, it is to love one another and to live as siblings with fellow Christians.

And the impact of love is tremendous. As McKnight points out, "Calling church people siblings means expecting that church folks will love *all* their church siblings and not just those of their own gender, age, or status."[41] This kind of love is a powerful witness to the world, as Jesus says: "By this everyone will know that you are my disciples, if you have love for one another" (John 13:35).

Strategies to Desexualize Workplace Culture

Changing workplace culture means changing attitudes and patterns of behavior. Research shows that changes in behavior can actually lead to changes in attitude, and it is much easier to establish behavioral standards and practices, which are visible, than to mandate attitudes, which are invisible and often unknowable, even to the individual.[42] So, start by implementing small workplace changes that show women are valued as colleagues and siblings, not seen as primarily sexual beings.

Use Inclusive Language

An easy place to start might be with language.[43] Some denominations and cultures routinely refer to each other as "brother" and "sister" at church. While that would not be appropriate in other types of organizations, it might work in a church setting. If the organization does choose this approach, accompany it with teaching about the biblical view of Christians as siblings in Christ.

In any organization, make sure the Bible translation being used makes "sisters" just as visible as "brothers." And make sure that inclusive language is used in sermons and messaging so that "sisters" can see themselves just as easily as "brothers" can.

41. McKnight, *Pastor Paul*, 65.
42. Chip Heath and Dan Heath, *Switch: How to Change Things When Change Is Hard* (Currency, 2010). The authors talk about change in terms of a rider (intellect), an elephant (emotions or attitudes), and a path (the mechanisms for change). Change happens best, they argue, when the path is clear and smooth, and reasons for change address both attitude and intellect.
43. See chap. 2 for more details on helpful and unhelpful uses of language.

Another strategy is to stop using the term "ladies" to refer to women in the workplace. "Lady" is technically a designation of social class and carries associations of leisure and privilege. In the workplace, it can feel off-putting since women are not present in order to be "ladies"; they are there to work. So refer to them as women, as colleagues, as coworkers, but not as ladies.

See Women as People, Not Relationships

In late 2024 a meme went around on social media that said, "Women get addressed by Miss, Mrs. or Ms. because society deems it important to know if [a woman] is single, married, or divorced. Men are only addressed by Mr. because their relationship to women does not affect their social status." And indeed, much of Western culture defines women based on their relationship to men.

In my research women describe being viewed as potential romantic partners, mothers, or daughters for their male colleagues. The problem with these views is that at work, women are not present as lover, mother, or daughter; they are coworkers focused on the same organizational tasks and goals. Women are full human beings of inherent value, not just valuable in their relationship roles to men. Therefore, guard against the tendency for these images to creep in at work. This chapter has focused primarily on the challenges with women being seen as potential romantic or sexual partners. However, the other two images can also be problematic.

Thinking of women at work as mother figures may lead to unconscious expectations of supportive and nurturing behavior. The result is expecting additional work from them, such as office housework, emotional support, and cheerleader-type behavior.[44] Women are not "work moms" for their colleagues; they are colleagues there to do their own jobs.

44. Diehl and Dzubinski, *Glass Walls*, 62, 96–98.

Thinking of women as daughter figures has the unintended consequence of diminishing them in terms of their perceived competence and capacity. Daughters may be protected by their fathers and as minors may be under their father's authority. But that is not the relationship in the workplace, even if the man is the woman's boss. He is still not her father, and the relationship is one of employer-employee, not parent-child. Women who are viewed as daughters are also likely to experience role incredulity and benevolent, possibly sanctified, sexism, which diminishes their agency and work satisfaction.[45]

Review and Update Policies

Make sure any policies take into consideration women's needs and desires as well as men's. Do a careful review of any policies where the stained-glass partition may be embedded in the form of the Pence/Graham rule. If travel with a colleague of the opposite sex is prohibited, make sure the policy provides equal access to funding and support for both women and men. Also think through travel in terms of safety and security for women. Are they at risk if they travel alone? Do they need to arrive and depart within daylight hours to ensure their security? Do not use reasons like those to exclude women from important travel. Instead, consider whether travel policies can be flexible based on location, purpose, and who is traveling. Some colleagues may be perfectly comfortable traveling together while others may not. A transparent conversation about expectations is healthier than inflexible rules. Any policies should be developed with the good of both women and men in mind.

---

45. Diehl and Dzubinski, *Glass Walls*, 107; Amy B. Diehl and Leanne M. Dzubinski, "When People Assume You're Not in Charge Because You're a Woman," *Harvard Business Review*, December 22, 2021, https://hbr.org/2021/12/when-people-assume-youre-not-in-charge-because-youre-a-woman. See chap. 4 for more on types of sexism.

Similarly, if the organization has an office romance policy, examine it carefully to ensure that men are not favored over women. Many workplaces have rules about dating one's co-worker. In some instances good, healthy marriages can result when single colleagues with similar values get to know one another through a Christian workplace. However, if a relationship ends, the results can range from awkward to toxic. Make sure the woman is not the only one responsible for handling any fallout or change required from a dating relationship that ends. Similarly, if an organizational policy prevents married couples from working in the same department or forbids one from reporting to the other, ensure that women are not by default the ones expected to transfer or quit if a couple decides to marry.

If your organization has no harassment policy, institute one. Find out what the legal requirements are in your area and work scrupulously to comply. If a policy exists, make sure women have a safe way to report harassment. Ensure everyone in the organization understands what constitutes harassment and what does not. Saying, "You look nice today" is not harassment, so do not joke that it is. But do remember that comments about physical appearance belong in the home, not the workplace. Be clear, take real harassment seriously, and do not trivialize it by pretending that normal interactions constitute harassment.

Breaking the Stained-Glass Partition

Applied as a hard-and-fast rule across the board, the stained-glass partition has more drawbacks than benefits. It is worth investing time and energy to create healthier ways of relating to one another. Organizational outcomes and employee satisfaction are likely to improve with wholesome workplace relationships. One good place to start is by emphasizing the biblical metaphor of siblings to explain relationships in the Christian workplace. As siblings, Christians belong to the same family and can jointly pursue the aims and goals of the organization.

Then work to find creative paths for mentoring, sponsoring, holding meetings, and conducting other forms of work. Do not simply impose the Pence/Graham rule on everyone. For one thing, a legalistic rule does not address heart issues and therefore will not, in most cases, be effective at stopping an inappropriate relationship if two people are determined to have one. Second, the rule has side effects that disproportionately disadvantage women. Also remember that men's and women's reasons for setting boundaries may be very different. Instead of enforcing a blanket rule, try having thoughtful conversations about organizational values and goals. Normalize cross-gender meetings and relationships by having more of them, not fewer. Encourage male and female colleagues to meet routinely to talk over work matters, chat over lunch, or work on projects. Make sure mentoring happens during work hours in established meeting spaces and is available to everyone in the organization. If individual cross-gender mentoring feels problematic, try mentoring in small groups rather than one-on-one.

Finally, provide nonjudgmental pathways for someone with a problem to get help. If an employee discloses that they have struggled in the past, whether from being abused or by engaging in wrong behavior, listen to them and take them seriously. Have policies and an HR system in place to help them create safe boundaries for themselves in ways that do not disadvantage others in their orbit or area of responsibility.

Chapter Summary

This chapter has tackled the problem of a sexualized workplace and the resulting stained-glass partition that may be created in an attempt to maintain appropriate relationships between men and women. It has explored the nature of the partition, men's and women's different reasons for sometimes wanting a partition, and the negative outcomes for women at work when the partition is enforced as a blanket norm. The chapter also looked at the Bible's solution to the problem of a sexualized culture: the view of fellow believers as brothers and sisters in Christ. An emphasis on sibling relationships, along with the recognition that believers are part of the body of Christ and are commanded to love one another as fellow heirs, is a good corrective to societal views of women as lovers, mothers, or daughters in relation to men. The chapter concluded with practical suggestions for breaking down the stained-glass partition to create a workplace culture where men and women can work well together and where women can thrive.

2

"Hey Guys!"

How Language Shapes Organizational Culture

Sticks and stones may break my bones, but words can never hurt me.

—common adage

Masculine nouns, such as "brothers" when the meaning is "brothers and sisters," effectively distance women from the text. I experienced this a while ago when I read the book of Hebrews in the ESV. It felt like nothing in Hebrews was relevant to me as a woman. It was unpleasant and disconcerting to feel distant from the Word of God that I love so much.

—Marg Mowczko, "Manhood and Masculinity in the ESV"

Can you remember a time when someone's words were particularly damaging to you? Or a time when someone's words were particularly helpful to you? I can remember both. First, the damaging words. My family was at a church picnic, and things were wrapping up for the day. My daughter was part of the worship team, and she walked up to another church member to inquire about the arrival time for Sunday morning. He said, "Shut up!" and added that, according to the Bible, women are to be silent. To clarify, she had not interrupted him in conversation, and he was not using a joking tone. I sent her to the car and had a talk with him about the inappropriateness of his words. Fortunately, my daughter does not remember the event, but I certainly do. Those words were terribly hurtful, and I struggle to understand how a church leader could speak to a young teen that way.

Helpful words can also have a tremendous impact for good in our lives. One time I was wrestling with a difficult decision and talked it over with a mentor. After going over all of the issues with me, rather than offer advice, he said, "I trust the Spirit of God in you." That short sentence had an amazing impact. It affirmed my discernment process, that I was listening to the Holy Spirit and seeking obedience. To this day I also remember his comment and the value of having someone listen and support me in a difficult time.

Language matters. Despite the saying about "sticks and stones" taught to children, the destructive power of words is evident in society and in life. Social media has amplified the reach of hurtful words, even leading some—teens and others—to self-harm as a result of online bullying.[1] It is impossible to overestimate the power of words, both to harm but also to

---

1. Ophely Dorol-Beauroy-Eustache and Brian L. Mishara, "Systematic Review of Risk and Protective Factors for Suicidal and Self-Harm Behavior Among Children and Adolescents Involved with Cyberbullying," *Preventive Medicine* 152, no. 1 (2021): 1; Ann John et al., "Self-Harm, Suicidal Behaviours, and Cyberbullying in Children and Young People: Systematic Review," *Journal of Medical Internet Research* 20, no. 4 (2018): 1–2.

heal.[2] Because words do matter, and words are powerful, how is it that Christians sometimes pay so little attention to their speech? And more specifically, why do Christians not think more about organizational communication?

In this chapter I will describe some organizational communication patterns that—unintentionally or perhaps intentionally—marginalize and alienate women. First is the use of masculine language as normative for all humans, and second is the challenge women have in getting their voices heard in meetings and public spaces. Both challenges contribute to women's sense of not belonging in the workplace, and both inhibit their flourishing. After unpacking the problems, I will offer some thoughts from the Bible and some concrete strategies that organizations can use to change their communication practices.

Masculine Language

The first language problem that creates challenges for women is "masculine language," meaning the use of terms like "he" or "guys" to mean "everyone."[3] Such language was fairly normal half a century ago. But language changes, and using masculine terms to refer to people generically is no longer normative in society, in education, or in any of the writing style guides students learn at school. So when Christian organizations continue to use such language, they create two problems. First, they sound old-fashioned and out of date. Second, they create an extra layer of work for any girls and women who are listening.

2. Kristen Hannah Seerig et al., "The Healing Power of Words: Examining the Effect of Communication Styles on Appreciation Within the Hospital Setting," *Procedia Computer Science* 231 (2024): 307.

3. Amy B. Diehl and Leanne M. Dzubinski, *Glass Walls: Shattering the Six Gender Bias Barriers That Still Hold Women Back at Work* (Rowman & Littlefield, 2023), 29; Amy B. Diehl, "'Guys' Is Not Gender-Neutral—Let's Stop Using It Like It Is," *Fast Company*, January 7, 2024, https://www.fastcompany.com/90629391/guys-is-not-gender-neutral-lets-stop-using-it-like-it-is.

It is hard to know which aspect of the problem is more serious. Sounding old-fashioned and out of date may be a turn-off to visitors and those outside the church community. It may be particularly harmful to young people, and the church is already struggling to retain them. Historically, men have been less connected to religion than women, but that is changing. According to a recent study by the Survey Center on American Life, the past twenty years have seen enormous numbers of people leaving churches and faith communities. And the pattern continued throughout 2024. The study found that among boomers who left the church, 57 percent were men and 43 percent were women; among millennials and Gen X, more men than women also left, although the percentages were shifting toward women. But as of Gen Z, the percentages have flipped. Now more women leave the faith than men. Moreover, the study found that 65 percent of the young women they polled "do not believe that churches treat men and women equally."[4] More than half of young men agreed. Of the older cohorts surveyed, half or more—both men and women—also noted unequal treatment. Masculine language is certainly not the only issue, but it may well be a factor in the perception of unequal treatment, and it likely contributes to women's sense that they do not fit in.

Second, when masculine language is used, it may create internal turmoil even in the most faithful woman at church, as she struggles to feel seen and heard by language that hides and silences her presence in the room. Using masculine language means that women have to go through a mental translation process of asking themselves, "Am I included in that comment,

4. Daniel A. Cox and Kelsey Eyre Hammond, "Young Women Are Leaving Church in Unprecedented Numbers," Survey Center on American Life, April 4, 2024, https://www.americansurveycenter.org/newsletter/young-women-are-leaving-church-in-unprecedented-numbers/.

or is it just for men who are listening?"[5] By the time they have figured out the answer, they may have lost the thread of the conversation. And whether that thread was a sermon or a conversation in a meeting, the damage is done.

Of course many women are still familiar with the old convention, even if they do not hear it in daily life. And women in church may be particularly accustomed to such language. However, the extra layer of work is still problematic. Although they may be able to do the internal translation required to figure out that "man" or "brothers" is meant to include them, they still encounter a barrier to understanding. Imagine a sermon based on James 1:26. A preacher using the ESV would read: "If anyone thinks he is religious and does not bridle his tongue but deceives his heart, this person's religion is worthless." Those who still remember the old way of talking may understand that both men and women are included in the exhortation. Younger women and girls, however, could mistakenly believe that the message is only for boys and men—because the rest of their world today makes it linguistically clear who is included and excluded in any given conversation.[6]

Language is alive and constantly changing.[7] New words come and go in our collective vocabulary; words change their meanings and fall into and out of favor. It is easy to get stuck on an old meaning and argue that it is "correct" and newer

---

5. Bill Mounce, *What I Have Learned About Greek and Translation Since Joining the CBT*, booklet, 2019, https://doxa.billmounce.com/What-I-Have-Learned-Bill-Mounce.pdf; Alice P. Mathews, *Preaching That Speaks to Women* (Baker Academic, 2003), 160.

6. Mounce, *What I Have Learned*, 26–27. Mounce tells the story of his eight-year-old daughter printing out a verse and then marking out "he" and writing "she." When he asked her about it, she said, "The Bible is for me too and not just [my brother], isn't it?" (27).

7. See, for example, this article about words popular in colonial America that have largely disappeared from present-day usage: Joe Gillard, "14 Colonial-Era Slang Terms to Work into Modern Conversation," Mental Floss, January 15, 2020, https://www.mentalfloss.com/article/612217/colonial-era-slang-terms.

usages are "incorrect." One phrase that is currently undergo-
ing a change of meaning is to say that something "begs the
question." Formerly, to "beg the question" meant to assume
the truth of the statement or to avoid answering it. But very
few people today use it that way. The meaning has shifted so
that the phrase now popularly means "leads one to ask the
question."[8] If I go around continuing to insist—in any but the
most formal settings—on the old usage, people are not going
to understand me. The phrase has changed meaning over the
years, and the only reasonable response is to learn the new
meaning. Language does change, and anyone who wants their
messages to stay comprehensible and relevant needs to change
their usage too.

If you are still tempted to think that using masculine language
is not such a big deal or that, even though language changes,
sticking with male words in church and Bible readings is okay,
consider some other words that have changed meaning or are
no longer used. How might single women in your organization
react to being called "spinsters," for example? Or consider the
word "senile," which used to mean things related to old age.
How would older members of your congregation like to be
called the "senile group"?[9] Think about the word "gay," which
used to mean "happy" or "carefree" but now is widely understood to refer to same-sex attraction. The *Merriam-Webster
Dictionary* still lists the meanings of "happy," "bright," and
"merry," but how likely are you to insist on using the term
that way in your organization?[10] That usage would create great
confusion.

8. *Merriam-Webster Dictionary*, "beg the question," accessed April 1, 2025,
https://www.merriam-webster.com/grammar/beg-the-question.
9. "20 Words That Once Meant Something Very Different," TED, June 18,
2014, https://ideas.ted.com/20-words-that-once-meant-something-very-different/.
10. *Merriam-Webster Dictionary*, "gay," accessed March 20, 2025, https://
www.merriam-webster.com/dictionary/gay.

In short, using outdated and unclear language marginalizes hearers who cannot find themselves in the message. Chesna Hinkley explains, "The word 'brethren' has no place in mixed company. Few things are more bitingly isolating than the realization that your humanity is so insignificant as to be subsumed into that of the man standing next to you."[11] Not only is using male language isolating for women, but it can come across as a deliberate slight. She explains further, "Now that male terminology for humanity is no longer strict grammatical convention, its use is necessarily intentional, and a statement in favor of the casual marginalization of women."[12] Hinkley is correct: Women and girls are now used to hearing themselves included at work and school, so when they are not included at church, they will believe that they are intentionally being left out. They will believe that the message of the church or of the Bible does not apply to them.

Bible Translations

Another potentially problematic area is Bible translations. Translation is as much art as science, since languages are not exact matches for one another in vocabulary or grammar. Translators must always make choices about how they want to approach their work and how best to represent a text written in one language to speakers of another language. Broadly speaking, there are two main approaches to Bible translation. The first approach prefers to take the original language and "replicat[e] the form of the Greek and Hebrew" closely, only making changes when necessary for understanding.[13]

11. Chesna Hinkley, "4 Ways Complementarian Churches Can Be Better for Women," *CBE International*, December 13, 2017, https://www.cbeinternational.org/resource/4-ways-complementarian-churches-can-be-better-women/.
12. Hinkley, "4 Ways."
13. Bill Mounce, "Do Formal Equivalent Translations Reflect a Higher View of Plenary, Verbal Inspiration?," paper presented at the Evangelical Theological Association annual meeting, Denver, CO, 2018, https://doxa.billmounce.com

This approach is called formal equivalence. According to Bill Mounce, the KVJ, RSV, NASB, and ESV are some versions that would be included in this category.[14] For example, the translators of the ESV explain in their preface: "The ESV is an 'essentially literal' translation that seeks as far as possible to capture the precise wording of the original text and the personal style of each Bible writer. As such, its emphasis is on 'word-for-word' correspondence, at the same time taking into account differences of grammar, syntax, and idiom between current literary English and the original languages."[15] That approach clearly falls within the formal-equivalence framework.

The second main approach is called "functional equivalence." Translations taking this approach emphasize "the meaning of each of the original words understood in context."[16] The focus in these translations is on meaning rather than on structures of Greek and Hebrew grammar and wording. Mounce places the NIV and NET into this category.[17] In the preface to the NIV, the translators explain, "The aim of the [translation] Committee is to put the Scriptures into natural English that will

---

/Inspiration_and_Translation_Theory.pdf, p. 2. Mounce argues for five approaches to translation. For the purposes of this book, two are sufficient. Readers may want to look at his five varieties.

14. Mounce, "Do Formal Equivalent Translations Reflect a Higher View?," 2.

15. See "Preface to the Standard English Version," https://www.esv.org/preface/. Mounce notes that they "invented" the term "essentially literal" as an alternative for "formal equivalence." Mounce, "Do Formal Equivalent Translations Reflect a Higher View?," 2.

16. Mounce, "Do Formal Equivalent Translations Reflect a Higher View?," 2. Kerr comments that Eugene Nida's description of "dynamic equivalence" is similar, though it goes one step further than functional equivalence. Dynamic equivalence is concerned with the reader's response to the translation, desiring that it be "substantially the same as that which existed between the original receptors and the message." Glenn J. Kerr, "Dynamic Equivalence and Its Daughters: Placing Bible Translation Theories in Their Historical Context," *Journal of Translation* 7, no. 1 (2011): 1.

17. The NET is inconsistent, however. See, for example, how they chose to translate James 1:26: "If someone thinks he is religious yet does not bridle his tongue, and so deceives his heart, his religion is futile."

communicate effectively with the broadest possible audience of English speakers."[18]

Because language is alive and ever-changing, and because translators and readers may prefer different approaches, both of these translation theories are useful. Formal equivalent translations offer readers a picture of what the original authors said to their audiences. Functional equivalent translations help modern readers understand what the original authors meant.

One area of challenge for translators in both traditions has to do with language and gender. And the two traditions have chosen distinctly different approaches. The ESV, in its pursuit of formal equivalence, chose to use male terms such as "brothers" even when the context is clear that women are also included, in which case they add a footnote saying "brothers and sisters."[19] Similarly, an indefinite pronoun like "anyone" is followed by "he," as in James 1:26. The NIV takes the opposite approach, using today's gender-accurate language when the text is clearly meant to include both men and women.[20] A gender-accurate translation "refers to 'men' using male language, 'women' using female language, and use[s] inclusive terms when referring to both men and women."[21] The impact of this choice on readers matters because, as already discussed, masculine language

18. "New International Version [NIV] Preface," Blue Letter Bible, https://www.blueletterbible.org/bibles/preface-to-the-new-international-version.cfm.
19. The ESV preface states, "A recurring note is included to indicate that the term "brothers" (*adelphoi*) was often used in Greek to refer to both men and women, and to indicate the specific instances in the text where this is the case." "Preface to the Standard English Version," https://www.esv.org/preface/.
20. The NIV preface states, "But the tendency, recognized in day-to-day usage . . . is away from the generic use of 'he,' 'him' and 'his.' In recognition of this shift in language and in an effort to translate into the natural English that people are actually using, this revision of the NIV generally uses other constructions when the biblical text is plainly addressed to men and women equally." "New International Version [NIV] Preface," Blue Letter Bible, https://www.blueletterbible.org/bibles/preface-to-the-new-international-version.cfm.
21. Mounce, *What I Have Learned*, 26.

distances women from the text and makes them question whether they are included.

Consider these translations of James 1:26:

NKJV: If anyone among you thinks he is religious, and does not bridle his tongue but deceives his own heart, this one's religion is useless.

ESV: If anyone thinks he is religious and does not bridle his tongue but deceives his heart, this person's religion is worthless.

NIV: Those who consider themselves religious and yet do not keep a tight rein on their tongues deceive themselves, and their religion is worthless.

NRSVue: If any think they are religious and do not bridle their tongues but deceive their hearts, their religion is worthless.

It seems obvious that the exhortation to watch one's speech is not meant exclusively for men (or women). Yet the NKJV and ESV pose an extra challenge for women readers, as they may not be quite sure if they are included or not.

Alternatively, take the same verses and use only female pronouns to see how that sounds. James 1:26 would read: "If anyone thinks she is religious and does not bridle her tongue but deceives her heart, this person's religion is worthless." Men reading that text would not be likely to think that it included them. So why expect women to believe they are included when only male pronouns are used? Gender-accurate translations are a useful tool for helping people grow in their faith, women and men alike.

External Organizational Communication

Communication problems are not limited to understanding Bible texts. They can also crop up in things like recruiting applicants for open positions. Studies show that women typically apply for a position only if they meet close to 100 percent of the required qualifications, whereas men will apply when they meet 60 percent.[22] Studies also show that certain words in job descriptions signal that the position is for men.[23] A job posting that uses words like "competitive" indicates a preference for men, and so does the use of masculine pronouns like "he" or "his" in describing qualifications and responsibilities. Masculine language, whether in the form of masculine pronouns or words that signal a preference for men to apply, means that the applicant pool will be reduced, and some qualified and gifted women may not apply because of these signals that their application would not be considered.

Another area of problematic organizational communication has to do with external communication through websites, newsletters, devotionals, and other organizational documents. If such documents use masculine language when all humans are meant, the organization creates barriers to understanding. Women and girls reading such communications may conclude that the ideas do not apply to them. If the communications rely on Bible texts that make women invisible, then women and girls may lose interest in the organization and its goals.

In sum, then, masculine language, although it used to be standard English, has steadily dropped out of usage over the last fifty-plus years. Some Christian organizations and churches, however, have been slow to adjust to this language change. Using outdated and inaccurate language negatively impacts women and girls, who may struggle to understand what is being communicated or to know whether it applies to them. It

22. Diehl and Dzubinski, *Glass Walls*, 28; Tara Sophia Mohr, "Why Women Don't Apply for Jobs Unless They're 100% Qualified," *Harvard Business Review*, August 25, 2014, https://hbr.org/2014/08/why-women-dont-apply-for-jobs-unless -theyre-100-qualified.
23. Diehl and Dzubinski, *Glass Walls*, 28.

communicates exclusion to them. If Christian organizations instead use gender-accurate language to make clear when men, women, and both are meant, it can reduce barriers for women and help them thrive.

Women Not Being Heard

The second major language problem in Christian organizations is more likely to occur in meetings than in sermons or job descriptions. It is the challenge women encounter, over and over again, of simply trying to get their voices and ideas heard in meetings.[24] Because of gender socialization, women are expected to talk in certain ways and men in other ways. Men are trained to be dominant while women are trained to be supportive and relational.[25] The outcome of this socialization is that women frequently report having difficulty getting themselves heard in a meeting or conversation.

In our research with over sixteen hundred women in four different industries—health care, law, higher education, and Christian organizations, Amy Diehl, Amber Stephenson, and I found that 80 percent or more women reported being careful when expressing authority, downplaying their accomplishments, and being cautious in speaking up. And over 50 percent reported being interrupted by men when they were talking.[26] These problems affect many women in many fields; in fact, challenges to women's communication may be the most common problem reported by women in any type of organizational setting.

24. Diehl and Dzubinski, *Glass Walls*, 49.

25. Deborah Tannen, "The Power of Talk: Who Gets Heard and Why," *Harvard Business Review* (September–October 1995): 140, https://hbr.org/1995/09/the-power-of-talk-who-gets-heard-and-why.

26. Amy B. Diehl et al., "Measuring the Invisible: Development and Multi-Industry Validation of the Gender Bias Scale for Women Leaders," *Human Resource Development Quarterly* 31, no. 3 [2020]: 269.

Consider this story from Donna, a mission leader:

I feel that women—it doesn't seem that men have to do this as much—do a lot of negotiating outside the normal meetings. I found I succeeded as a leader by actually having these outside conversations, knowing that if I mentioned something in a meeting it wouldn't have the same credibility it might if a man mentioned it, or a certain man. So I would have conversations with those individuals and influence them enough to where either they supported me when I brought something up, or they actually brought it up themselves. And I had to accept the fact that that was just the way one worked.[27]

Rather than walking into a meeting ready to share her ideas with the rest of the team, she had to work behind the scenes in advance just to get a hearing. In the years since she told me that story, a number of words have entered our collective vocabulary to describe the various challenges women run into while speaking.

First came "mansplaining," which means "to explain something to a woman in a condescending way that assumes she has no knowledge about the topic."[28] The problem was first described by Rebecca Solnit in her essay "Men Explain Things to Me."[29] In it she describes how a man spent significant time describing her own book to her, while she and her friend fruitlessly tried to tell him that she was the author of said book. Now mansplaining refers to any time a man starts informing a woman about something she already knows, and it is one of numerous ways men dominate conversations even when they have less to contribute.

27. Leanne M. Dzubinski, "Taking on Power: Women Leaders in Evangelical Mission Organizations," *Missiology: An International Review* 44, no. 3 (2016): 288.

28. *Merriam-Webster Dictionary*, "mansplain," accessed March 20, 2025, https://www.merriam-webster.com/dictionary/mansplain.

29. Rebecca Solnit, "Men Explain Things to Me," *Guernica*, August 20, 2012, https://www.guernicamag.com/rebecca-solnit-men-explain-things-to-me/.

Another term that has entered our collective vocabulary is "hepeat." Hepeating happens when a woman says something in a meeting and it is ignored, then the statement is repeated by a man and praised.[30] The great idea is then credited to the man, not to the woman who came up with it in the first place.

The next word is "bropropriate," which is when a man repeats a woman's contribution and actively takes credit for it as his own. It is more intentional than hepeating and has the same negative outcome for the woman.[31] It looks like the man has contributed the great idea, even though it originated with the woman.

Then there is "mantermediary," meaning that a woman intentionally uses a man as an intermediary to present her ideas.[32] Typically she uses this strategy because she has a good idea and wants it to be heard, but she knows that she has little chance of gaining a hearing for herself. Perhaps she has been silenced so thoroughly and so often that she has given in to the limitations she encounters.[33] So she finds a male colleague and persuades him to present the idea for her, or even as his own, as Donna described.

Finally, there is "manterrupt," which happens when a man needlessly interrupts a woman while she is presenting her ideas.[34] Interrupting is both rude and disrespectful, yet men do it to women frequently. Gender socialization of men to be

30. Andrea Park, "The Internet Is Loving This New Word for When a Man Repeats Your Idea and Gets Credit," Allure, September 25, 2017, https://www.allure.com/story/hepeat-twitter-reactions. See also Diehl and Dzubinski, Glass Walls, 50.

31. Jessica Bennett, "How Not to Be 'Manterrupted' in Meetings," Time, January 20, 2015, https://time.com/3666135/sheryl-sandberg-talking-while-female-manterruptions/. See also Diehl and Dzubinski, Glass Walls, 50–51.

32. In Glass Walls, we discuss coining a number of terms for women's experiences of bias that had previously been unnamed. "Mantermediary" is one of them. See Diehl and Dzubinski, Glass Walls, 7–8, 174–75.

33. Diehl and Dzubinski, Glass Walls, 161.

34. Bennett, "How Not to Be 'Manterrupted.'"

dominant and women submissive creates a climate where men interrupting women is not seen as problematic. Yet it is problematic. Interrupting a woman is a way of silencing her and discounting her ideas. It may also be a form of shaming, implying that women should be quiet.

The problem with all of these types of communication is that women do not get credit for their own ideas. In each case, the idea is received as someone else's, not hers. And that perception can diminish her apparent value and what she is seen as contributing to the team or organization. Over time this loss of value can even lead to her being asked to step off the team. Trying to speak up when her ideas are hijacked may not necessarily work either. Because of gender socialization, if women speak up and try to take credit for their own ideas, they may encounter backlash. Backlash is "the negative evaluation of agentic women for violating prescriptions of feminine niceness."[35] Put another way, backlash happens when women are criticized for not conforming to gendered expectations of being supportive and submissive, valuing everyone else before themselves.

In summary, women simply face additional obstacles to communication that men do not encounter. The combined effect of these challenges that women face in getting their voices heard is that, at the end of the day, women are silenced. Sometimes they are literally told to shut up, as my daughter was.[36] Other times they are silenced and excluded from the conversation by less drastic, but equally successful, means.

Where Did Preferences for Women's Silence Originate?

Unfortunately, this silencing of women has a long history that is rooted in Greek society and has also permeated the

---

35. Laurie A. Rudman and Peter Glick, "Prescriptive Gender Stereotypes and Backlash Toward Agentic Women," *Journal of Social Issues* 57, no. 4 (2001): 743.

36. For stories of women being told to shut up at work, see Diehl and Dzubinski, *Glass Walls*, 57–59.

church for many centuries. The idea has been promoted by various philosophers and religious teachers from the ancient Greeks right up to the present. Aristotle, for example, is known for viewing men as superior to women.[37] He seems to promote women's silence too, quoting Sophocles's saying: "To woman, silence is an adornment."[38]

Some of the most revered reformers of the church also promoted ideas of women's silence. Martin Luther, for example, both promoted the ancient Greek ideas regarding women and simultaneously treated women close to him well, relying heavily on his wife Katarina's capabilities. Yet he also encouraged her, and all women, to talk less.[39] John Knox promoted a preference for women's silence in his treatise published in 1558.[40] And a collection of sermons from the fifteenth century by Johannes Mirkus contains this teaching: "A mayde schuld be seen but not herd."[41]

More recently, complementarian teachers continue to promote the idea that women should not preach or teach publicly.[42] One leader even commented that men should not speak at Christian conferences that include women: "When you have men and women preachers. I can't do that."[43] Although most

---

37. Leanne M. Dzubinski and Anneke H. Stasson, *Women in the Mission of the Church: Their Opportunities and Obstacles Throughout Christian History* (Baker Academic, 2021), 2.

38. Dana Jalbert Stauffer, "Aristotle's Account of the Subjection of Women," *The Journal of Politics* 70, no. 4 (2008): 937.

39. *Luther on Women: A Sourcebook*, trans. Susan C. Karant-Nunn and Merry E. Wiesner-Hanks (Cambridge University Press, 2003), 10.

40. John Knox, *The First Blast of the Trumpet Against the Monstrous Regiment of Women* (London: 1558), https://www.gutenberg.org/files/9660/9660-h/9660-h.htm.

41. In today's English it would say "A girl should be seen but not heard." Johannes Mirkus, *Mirk's Festival: A Collection of Homilies*, ed. Theodor Erbe (Kegan Paul, 1905), 230.

42. For such arguments see https://cbmw.org.

43. Julie Roys, "John MacArthur Tells Seminarians Not to Speak at Conferences with Women, Even Though He Has," *The Roys Report*, May 8, 2023, https://julieroys.com/john-macarthur-tells-seminarians-not-to-speak-at-conferences-with-women-even-though-he-has/.

complementarian teachers limit such prohibitions on women's speaking to the church, attitudes become ingrained and get acted on in other settings as well. Research has shown that religious beliefs about women can show up as sexist beliefs more generally.[44] Men are not the only ones affected either. Women who receive these kinds of teachings are more likely to have sexist beliefs as well.[45] That church leader who told my daughter to shut up was simply acting on a long-standing, mistaken tradition that women's silence is God's design.

Scripture's Perspective

In this section I will take a look at what the Bible says about communication in the family of Christ. The Bible is full of instructions about how to talk with one another. Some instruction is positive, and other passages are warnings about the negative consequences of careless or harmful talk. But before looking at those passages, I want to consider some tricky passages about women's quietness or silence in the church.

First Timothy 2:1–15 is perhaps one of the stickiest passages in all of the biblical text. It is riddled with exegetical and lexical challenges. The purpose here is not to examine the entire passage. For help with unpacking the whole section, see Philip Payne's work *The Bible vs. Biblical Womanhood*.[46] The salient verses for our topic are verses 11–12: "A woman should learn in quietness and full submission. I do not permit a woman to teach or to assume authority over a man; she must be quiet"

---

44. Małgorzata Mikołajczak and Janina Pietrzak, "Ambivalent Sexism and Religion: Connected Through Values," *Sex Roles* 70 (2014): 387–99.

45. Kristen Davis Eliason et al., "Where Gender and Religion Meet: Differentiating Gender Role Ideology and Religious Beliefs About Gender," *Journal of Psychology and Christianity* 36, no. 1 (2017): 3–15.

46. Philip Barton Payne, *The Bible vs. Biblical Womanhood: How God's Word Consistently Affirms Gender Equality* (Zondervan, 2023). Chapter 10 is devoted to this passage.

(NIV). That is how the translators of the NIV used functional equivalence to translate those verses. The translators of the ESV, a formal-equivalence translation, used this wording: "Let a woman learn quietly with all submissiveness. I do not permit a woman to teach or to exercise authority over a man; rather, she is to remain quiet." Interestingly, both approaches landed on forms of "submissive" and "quiet" as the correct ideas in this text, rather than "silence" as used in the King James Version and the New King James Version.

The purpose of verse 11 is to command women to learn, rather than to remain ignorant and susceptible to the false teachers that were harming the church in Ephesus—the very reason Paul had sent Timothy there in the first place.[47] Payne explains, "'Learn' here is an imperative. Paul commands that women must learn. He is not merely giving advice about the manner in which women should learn. This is the only imperative verb in this chapter."[48] Therefore, the focus of the command is women learning sound doctrine. The modifiers are not about absolute silence but about listening and submitting to sound teaching, the appropriate attitude of any learner at the time.[49] In Jewish tradition of the time, men learned from rabbis, but there was no standard method for women to learn. Paul's focus on women learning, therefore, is new and critical for the health of the church.

The next passage that is sometimes used to silence women is 1 Corinthians 14:34, which says, "Women should be silent in the churches." That is the verse that the worship leader used to bludgeon my daughter. An important consideration in seeking to understand this passage is that verse 34 is the third time, not the first, that Paul has commanded quietness. In verse 28 he states that if there is no one to interpret, the one speaking in

---

47. See 1 Tim. 1, where Paul instructs Timothy in his responsibilities.
48. Payne, *The Bible vs. Biblical Womanhood*, 142.
49. Payne, *The Bible vs. Biblical Womanhood*, 142.

tongues should be silent. In verse 30 he adds that if a second person receives a revelation, the first one should be silent. The focus of all his instructions in this chapter is order in the worship service. Taking turns speaking, being silent by turns, and paying attention to one another are all part of conducting an orderly service of worship. Verse 34, then, is not a blanket prohibition on women speaking but part of a series of exhortations for temporary quietness leading to an orderly worship service.

Another possibility is presented by Payne. After extensive study, his argument is that 1 Corinthians 14:34–35 is not original to Paul but represents an early marginal note written by a scribe that was later added to the text. In addition to textual evidence, Payne cites Greek law that required "women to be silent in public meetings."[50] He also points out that there is no scriptural law forbidding women to speak.[51] According to Beth Allison Barr, however, there were Roman arguments that women should be silent.[52] Furthermore, the entire text of the chapter up to these verses is addressed to everyone in the church, encouraging them to speak in tongues, prophesy, and pray.[53] So to then silence women makes no sense.

Thus, to interpret this one passage as mandating complete silence for all women in all churches at all times is to ignore clear statements throughout the Bible that women did and are expected to speak, prophesy, praise, sing, and otherwise engage verbally in worship at church. For many women in Christian organizations today, however, the problem is not one of extremes

50. Payne, *The Bible vs. Biblical Womanhood*, 83. See chap. 5 for his complete argument.

51. Payne, *The Bible vs. Biblical Womanhood*, 81.

52. Beth Allison Barr, *The Making of Biblical Womanhood: How the Subjugation of Women Became Gospel Truth* (Brazos, 2021), 59–60. According to Barr, these verses in 1 Corinthians closely resemble a speech given by Cato and recorded by Livy. Paul may well have known the speech and been quoting it in this text in order to refute it (59–61).

53. Both the ESV and the NIV use language showing that these gifts were not limited to men in the church.

but one of subtle exclusion and marginalization, as already discussed, through the use of masculine language and patterns of communication that favor men. What does the Bible have to say about these kinds of issues?

Fundamentally, the problem is about the marginalization of women and not caring about their perspectives and feelings. When women explain that reading the Bible feels alienating, or that sermons are hard to understand or off-putting, or that meetings and classrooms are frustrating because they cannot get their voices heard, how do their brothers in Christ respond to them? Do they listen? Do they believe women? Do they take these concerns seriously? Too often the answer is no. They may downplay the problem or tell women to be more assertive (but remember the backlash effect) and less sensitive. None of those approaches actually helps solve the problem. But the Bible is full of advice and instructions about speaking and the importance of hearing one another. Consider, for example, Proverbs 18:2, which states, "A fool takes no pleasure in understanding, / but only in expressing personal opinion." A man who insists on his own perspective, whether by pushing his own voice or by failing to take his sister seriously, is neglecting the good advice of this proverb. Similarly, a man who fails to remember Proverbs 15:4 ("A gentle tongue is a tree of life, / but perverseness in it breaks the spirit") may well be damaging his sister in Christ. The book of James puts it perhaps more strongly: "If any think they are religious and do not bridle their tongues but deceive their hearts, their religion is worthless" (1:26). Failing to listen to and take seriously women's experiences may well be considered a form of "deceiving one's heart"; similarly, continuing to talk rather than helping create space for women's contributions could well be a form of "not bridling one's tongue," which James 1:26 views as distinctly problematic. Shutting down one's colleagues and fellow believers, whether actively or passively, does not align with scriptural values.

Those who do pay attention to their own speaking and to others around them, however, are praised. Consider Proverbs 16:23–24, which explains:

> The mind of the wise makes their speech judicious
> and adds persuasiveness to their lips.
> Pleasant words are like a honeycomb,
> sweetness to the soul and health to the body.

How much better for women, for men, and for organizations, would it be if men's voices were "judicious" rather than dominating and if women's voices were truly heard and their wisdom incorporated into organizational decision-making? It could work if more people took 1 Peter 3:8 seriously: "Finally, all of you, have unity of spirit, sympathy, love for one another, a tender heart, and a humble mind." Or think of Philippians 2:3: "Do nothing from selfish ambition or empty conceit, but in humility regard others as better than yourselves." Humility—men regarding their own thoughts as no more valuable than the thoughts of women on the team—could go a long way toward rectifying the communication divide at work.

Strategies to Watch Your Language at Work

Strategies to create change in the area of language are relatively straightforward. They mostly are about making decisions to do things differently and then following through. Here I offer several strategies organizational leaders can use to create change.

Think About Masculine Language

Start by thinking about masculine language. What do your organizational documents communicate to readers? Do they use language that is easily understood today? Or do they sound outdated? If masculine pronouns are used when all people are meant, create updated documents with gender-accurate language. If you use historic documents that were written in a time when linguistic conventions were different, add a preface noting that language has changed and that current readers should understand masculine language to include both men and women.

Audit Job Descriptions and Advertisements

You can also do an audit of job descriptions and job advertisements. What kind of language is used? Are masculine pronouns signaling incorrectly that a position is not open to women? Are there code words like "competitive" or "aggressive" that might communicate to women that they should not apply? Think carefully about what you intend to indicate in job descriptions and advertisements, and make sure your language matches your intent.

Consider Bible Translations

Consider which Bible translations are used in official organizational communications to constituents, stakeholders, donors, alumni, and others. Are translations being used that communicate to women that they belong? Or is there an unintentional message of exclusion? While formal-equivalence Bible translations can be helpful for in-depth exegetical study, they can miscommunicate on Sunday morning or in organizational communication. If you choose to use a formal equivalent for some purposes, be sure to help hearers understand when such language is meant to include women. But be careful about only using such translations and relying on disclaimers to communicate a different message. Over time, the impact of hearing masculine language as biblical language takes a toll on women listeners. Repeated disclaimers may sound insincere, and women may well wonder why an organization insists on using a translation that intentionally excludes them. A better strategy is to use formal equivalence for personal study, and functional equivalence for public communication. For organizational members who hold strong preferences for a favorite translation, help them understand the difficulties for others while respecting their own traditions.

Examine Organizational Communication

Pay close attention to meeting communication styles. Spend a week tracking who speaks, for how long, how many interruptions happen, and how women respond if they are interrupted or talked over. Then bring the issue to the attention of your team. Build in expectations that interruptions will not be tolerated and that people will be able to finish their thoughts. Of course, you will still have to manage those who dominate, but ensure that what counts as domination is not gendered. A man speaking for five minutes may be tolerated, while a woman may be viewed as "dominating" after two minutes. Do not let those perceptions determine how conversations are managed.

Develop Allies

You can also build in ally strategies for meetings and communication. Teach others to support a woman's contributions and to call one another out if they hepeat, bropropriate, or manterrupt. If a woman—or a man—supports another woman's point, thank that person for their support. Consider appointing someone, on a rotating basis, to observe the conversations in every meeting. Authorize that person to call attention to issues of communication injustice and to hand the floor back to the woman making the original comment.

With the possible exception of using a different Bible translation in a church that is very used to a certain one, most of these changes are not difficult. They will require intentionality and follow-through, yet the results from small efforts are likely to be quite noticeable. Women will contribute more to organizational conversations. They will feel included, valued, and seen. Women in church will be more engaged. The whole Christian body will benefit from hearing and seeing all its members.

Chapter Summary

This chapter has looked at patterns of communication that can be alienating for women in Christian workplaces. First is the use of masculine language such as "he" that renders women invisible. Bible translations can be especially problematic when they intentionally use masculine language, leaving women to figure out whether or not they are included. The chapter also looked at organizational communication patterns that make it hard for women to get their ideas heard. Then it considered some of the tough Bible passages which, read superficially, appear to support women's silence. Yet careful exegesis and reading the full context makes it clear that the Bible does not command women's silence; instead, it commends judicious speech from everyone. The chapter concluded with strategies to communicate inclusion to women and enable women to contribute to organizational conversations, ensuring they, and the organizations they serve, can flourish.

3

"I Can't. I Have to Work."

The Toxic Cocktail of Societal Expectations

Women can learn to lead, but it comes more naturally to men. Some jobs just naturally fit women's skills better than men's skills.

If one parent needs to quit working, it makes more sense for the man to keep his job.

When it comes to tough decisions, men tend to have abilities that women don't have.

—ideology statements posed for participants to rate on a Likert scale[1]

Have you ever heard, or perhaps made, comments like these at work? What do you think about a colleague who always leaves on time, preferring not to stay late? How do

---

1. Statements adapted from Andrea L. Miller and Eugene Borgida, "The Separate Spheres Model of Gendered Inequality," *PLoS ONE* 11, no. 1 (2016): 31.

you respond to a colleague who leaves work early to take their child to the doctor but catches up on tasks later that evening at home? Does your opinion change if it is a man or a woman in the scenario?

Many organizations, supervisors, and employees frown on workers who stick closely to the workday schedule rather than being flexible around leaving (the first scenario) or who adjust their work schedule around caretaking needs (the second scenario). These scenarios make visible two strongly embedded expectations in US society around work and work culture. The first expectation is that an employee is always available: able to stay late, arrive early, work weekends, break their vacation if they are wanted at work, and so on. The second expectation is that an employee has someone else in their life who can take care of all personal and caretaking needs, which could include anything from caring for children, elderly parents, and friends or relatives with disabilities or illnesses to providing food and clothing, doing laundry, doing yard work, and more.

These unspoken expectations are deeply embedded in US culture. In this chapter I describe five core underlying beliefs about work that often go unnoticed and unquestioned. They are the ideal worker belief, greedy institutions, separate spheres, gender essentialism, and the two-person career structure. Each of these cultural beliefs, taken on its own, can appear innocuous or even positive. Yet taken together they create a toxic cocktail of expectations that make it very difficult for women to flourish at work. I will describe each of them in turn, then show how they combine into a recipe for discouragement. Then I will examine these expectations in light of biblical texts and offer practical suggestions for organizational leaders to start the process of organizational culture change.

The Ideal Worker

The expectation that an employee is always available for the organization and will never be distracted by other responsibilities because someone else in their life takes care of all such needs is known as the "ideal worker" belief. It was so named by Joan Acker in 1990; she defined an ideal worker as "the male worker whose life centers on his full-time, life-long job, while his wife or another woman takes care of his personal needs and his children."[2] Interestingly, she noted that this view was an ideal, not an actual reality for anyone. She also noted that women were "assumed to have legitimate obligations other than those required by the job" and so did not fit the ideal.[3]

Despite being unreal and unrealistic, data shows that Americans continue to work long hours in keeping with the ideal worker image. While Japan has long been known for its work culture and expectation that employees will put in long hours, Japanese and American workers now put in about the same average number of hours per year, and more hours than European workers.[4] People "glamourise" and "romanticize" overwork and think that working excessive hours is a "status symbol," says Bryan Rufkin.[5] One part of the challenge in the US is the lack of vacation time: "The US is the only *industrialized* country in the world that doesn't have legally mandated annual leave and doesn't guarantee its workers paid vacation."[6]

---

2. Joan Acker, "Hierarchies, Jobs, Bodies: A Theory of Gendered Organizations," *Gender & Society* 4, no. 2 (1990): 149.

3. Acker, "Hierarchies, Jobs, Bodies," 149.

4. "Average Working Hours (Statistical Data 2025)," Clockify, accessed March 21, 2025, https://clockify.me/working-hours; Bryan Rufkin, "Why Do We Buy into the 'Cult' of Overwork?," Worklife, *BBC*, May 9, 2021, https://www.bbc.com/worklife/article/20210507-why-we-glorify-the-cult-of-burnout-and-overwork.

5. Rufkin, "Why Do We Buy into the 'Cult' of Overwork?"

6. "Average Working Hours (Statistical Data 2025)." The lack of vacation is a bigger problem than I can discuss here. Organizations would do well to have a vacation policy and have leaders model using their vacation time to truly disconnect from work.

Another part of the challenge is how organizations are built and expected to function.

Greedy Institutions

Back in the 1970s, sociologist Lewis Coser identified what he called "greedy institutions." He said that they "seek exclusive and undivided loyalty" and that they do not want their members to engage in competing roles or carry out competing responsibilities.[7] As he put it, greedy institutions "are not content with claiming a segment of the energy of individuals but demand their total allegiance."[8] It is worth noting that he included priests and housewives in his original list of victims of greedy organizations. Since then, others have expanded his work to broaden the understanding of greedy institutions. For example, churches have been called greedy institutions because they demand "high levels of time, energy, money, and allegiance, and in some cases perhaps [strain] members' commitments to family, work, or other activities."[9] Churches are not the only organizations that fit this model, of course. Other researchers have identified greedy institutions such as the military,[10] universities[11] (particularly the "pandemic

---

7. Marshall W. Meyer, "Reviewed Work: *Greedy Institutions: Patterns of Undivided Commitment* by Lewis A. Coser," *American Journal of Sociology* 80, no. 6 (1975): 1495.

8. Lewis A. Coser, "Greedy Organizations," *European Journal of Sociology* 8, no. 2 (1967): 198.

9. Christopher G. Ellison and Jinwoo Lee, "Spiritual Struggles and Psychological Distress: Is There a Dark Side of Religion?," *Social Indicators Research* 98 (2010): 504.

10. Mady Wechsler Segal, "The Military and the Family as Greedy Institutions," *Armed Forces and Society* 13, no. 1 (1986): 9–38; Eiko Strader and Margaret Smith, "Some Parents Survive and Some Don't: The Army and the Family as 'Greedy Institutions,'" *Public Administration Review* 82, no. 3 (2022): 448.

11. Mary C. Wright et al., "Greedy Institutions: The Importance of Institutional Context for Teaching in Higher Education," *Teaching Sociology* 32, no. 2 (2004): 144.

university"[12]), family,[13] the police,[14] banks,[15] and hospitals.[16] Undoubtedly there are more.

Greedy institutions share some common characteristics. They expect loyalty, commitment, and compliance to organizational norms and culture.[17] They want full involvement of their members.[18] And they want compliance and involvement to be willingly given. Jan Currie, Patricia Harris, and Bev Thiele explain, "There is something about their nature which attracts voluntary compliance. Individuals assent to their lifestyle because it is highly attractive to them. In their turn, greedy institutions encourage their members to devote their total energies to collective tasks."[19]

The fight between workplaces and families as greedy institutions is particularly problematic for women. Elise Hu explains, "We're fed this notion that we should parent like we don't work and work like we don't parent. . . . It's ridiculous."[20] She is right: Since society tacitly endorses both the ideal worker myth and the greedy institution framing of work and family, it is ridiculous to expect women to fulfill both. Yet rather than challenge the unrealistic expectations, it falls to women

12. Molly Dingel et al., "Service, Self-Care, and Sacrifice: A Qualitative Exploration of the Pandemic University as a Greedy Institution," *Advance* 2, no. 3 (2021): 7.

13. Strader and Smith, "Some Parents Survive and Some Don't," 448.

14. Abby Peterson and Sara Uhnoo, "The Problem of Loyalty in Greedy Institutions," in *Psychology of Loyalty*, ed. L. B. Miller and W. C. Moore (Nova Science Publishers, 2013).

15. Rosaria Burchielli, Timothy Bartram, and Rani Thanacoody, "Work-Family Balance or Greedy Organizations?," *Industrial Relations* 63, no. 1 (2008): 124.

16. Burchielli, Bartram, and Thanacoody, "Work-Family Balance?," 124.

17. Peterson and Uhnoo, "Problem of Loyalty," 38; Burchielli, Bartram, and Thanacoody, "Work-Family Balance?," 112.

18. Burchielli, Bartram, and Thanacoody, "Work-Family Balance?," 112.

19. Jan Currie, Patricia Harris, and Bev Thiele, "Sacrifices in Greedy Universities: Are They Gendered?," *Gender and Education* 12, no. 3 (2000): 270.

20. Quoted in Claire Trageser, "Stop Telling Women They're Amazing," *Elle*, February 24, 2021, https://www.elle.com/life-love/a35562291/stop-telling-women-theyre-amazing/.

to negotiate between them and figure out how to handle the perpetual sense of failure.

Now, let's return to the idea of the ideal worker as someone who is available around the clock for their greedy institution. Remember, Joan Acker said it described men who had a wife to take care of all personal and family responsibilities, and she also said it was not a reality. So why do so many workplaces, including Christian ones such as churches, ministries, and Christian higher education institutions, continue to operate as if this model reflects appropriate Christian values? A brief look at history may help explain the origins of this thinking.

Separate Spheres

One of the social outcomes of the eighteenth century's industrial revolution was the development of what became known as "separate spheres" for men and women. Although upper-class Greek and Roman societies operated under a perspective of market and domestic realms, with men assigned to the market and women to the domestic realm, it was the industrial revolution that began in 1760 that re-created that system and set it up as the ideal aspirational standard for all families.

In nonindustrialized societies, work and home are often largely the same. Families run farms, small businesses, or shops to sell their handmade products. In the case of businesses and shops, the shop and the home often occupy parts of the same space. Children grow up seeing and learning the trade of their parents as the whole family works together.[21]

The industrial revolution changed that model for much of the world by steadily moving work out of the home and into factories and offices. In order to make a living, families needed

21. Alice P. Mathews, *Preaching That Speaks to Women* (Baker Academic, 2003), 160.

both parents and most children to take factory jobs. Only the wealthiest families could afford to have just the man working outside the home, with women and children remaining in the domestic sphere. According to Alice Mathews and Gay Hubbard, a one-earner household signaled entrance to the middle class, yet "at no time in the eighteenth and nineteenth centuries did the middle class comprise more than 10 percent of the American population."[22] Nevertheless, this division of labor and promotion of the idea that men belong in the public sphere of work and women in the private, domestic sphere became the idealized standard for family life. Historians have named it "the Victorian doctrine of separate spheres."[23] The appropriate role for women, in this doctrine, was "piety, purity, submissiveness, and domesticity" as they cared for the private realm of the home.[24] The appropriate sphere for men was the "world of work outside the home."[25] These ideas were a response to the changing nature of work and society, which separated families based on economic necessity. They were accepted by social and religious leaders of the time and widely promoted through sermons, theological journals, women's magazines, and other communications as the ideal for everyone. Evangelical faith, in particular, accepted and strongly promoted this vision starting in the late 1700s.[26]

In the twenty-first century, this value system continues to be readily apparent. In some evangelical spaces it is still taught and preached as the ideal "division of labor" for humanity. And while many evangelicals may accept that women need to be

---

22. Alice P. Mathews and M. Gay Hubbard, *Marriage Made in Eden: A Pre-Modern Perspective for a Post-Modern World* (Baker Books, 2004), 100.

23. Mathews and Hubbard, *Marriage Made in Eden*, 92.

24. Mathews and Hubbard, *Marriage Made in Eden*, 93.

25. Cathy Ross, "Separate Spheres or Shared Dominions?," *Transformation* 23, no. 4 (2006): 228. Ross points out that according to Aileen Kraditor, men don't really have a "sphere" since they have access to everything.

26. Ross, "Separate Spheres or Shared Dominions?," 228–29; Mathews and Hubbard, *Marriage Made in Eden*, 92–93, 102–4. They include a sample sermon on p. 103.

gainfully employed outside the home for the good of the family, the belief that the home and family are primarily women's responsibility persists with remarkable strength.[27]

However, this idealized vision of labor is not specific to Christian realms. Rather, Christian thinking resembles wider American culture. Andrea Miller and Eugene Borgida explain, "The general notion of separate spheres for men and women is deeply ingrained in our culture. Journalists, legal scholars, and social scientists have observed a wide variety of gendered phenomena that seem to be manifestations of the public's insistence that men and women occupy separate spheres."[28] They continue: "A common theme . . . is the idea that men and women belong in distinct spheres of society, with men being particularly fit for the workplace and women being particularly fit for the domestic domain."[29] What is interesting in their statement is the idea of "fit": Men are "fit" or suited for the area of paid work, and women are "fit" or suited for the area of unpaid household work. What do they mean by "fit"?

Gender Essentialist Thinking

Underlying the idea of "fit" is an assumption, popular in US society as well as in evangelicalism, that "men and women are innately and fundamentally different."[30] Beliefs that such dif-

---

27. See, for example, the research done by Lisa Weaver Swartz comparing Southern Seminary's Baptist, complementarian teaching with Asbury Theological Seminary's Wesleyan, egalitarian teaching. Although the two institutions differ significantly in their theological positions on women's ministry leadership, both emphasize the importance of women's role as wife and mother. Lisa Weaver Swartz, "Gendered Gospel, Ungendered Mission: Identity Construction at Two Evangelical Seminaries" (PhD diss., University of Notre Dame, 2017).

28. Miller and Borgida, "Separate Spheres Model," 2–3.

29. Miller and Borgida, "Separate Spheres Model," 2.

30. Patricia Homan and Amy Burdette, "When Religion Hurts: Structural Sexism and Health in Religious Congregations," *American Sociological Review* 86, no. 2 (2021): 238.

ferences between men and women are "innate" or "natural" is a form of gender essentialism, meaning "the belief in an underlying, unchangeable essence that defines a person, category, or thing."[31] Gender is often thought of in essentialist terms by those who believe that the differences between men and women are biological, not learned, and that they transcend culture and time.[32] Some typical essentialist beliefs would be that women are always more emotional than men, or that men are always more competitive than women.[33] Statements such as the ones that opened this chapter (e.g., "Some jobs just naturally fit women's skills better than men's skills") reflect essentialist thinking.

But essentialist thinking about gender has several problems. For one thing, expectations about how men and women should behave, think, and dress are culturally and historically conditioned, not innate. For example, some Asian cultures expect a good person to be able to know, intuitively, what another person is thinking and feeling, whereas US culture expects that sensitivity of women but not of men.[34] Or consider the topic of appropriate attire for babies. In the late 1880s in the US, white skirts, long hair, and patent leather shoes were considered gender neutral, though today those baby portraits look decidedly feminine.[35] The choices were practical: White was easy to launder, and cutting

31. Leanne M. Dzubinski and Amy B. Diehl, "The Problem of Gender Essentialism and Its Implications for Women in Leadership," *Journal of Leadership Studies* 12, no. 1 (2018): 56. Essentialist thinking is not limited to gender. Race and ethnicity are also sometimes thought of in essentialist terms.

32. Nick Haslam, Louis Rothschild, and Donald Ernst, "Essentialist Beliefs About Social Categories," *British Journal of Social Psychology* 39, no. 1 (2000): 114.

33. Dzubinski and Diehl, "Problem of Gender Essentialism," 56.

34. Erin Meyer, *The Culture Map: Breaking Through the Invisible Boundaries of Global Business* (PublicAffairs, 2014), 33–34.

35. Jeanne Maglaty, "When Did Girls Start Wearing Pink?," *Smithsonian Magazine*, April 7, 2011, https://www.smithsonianmag.com/arts-culture/when -did-girls-start-wearing-pink-1370097/. The Smithsonian article includes many fascinating portraits of boys and girls from previous generations.

a small child's hair was risky. When pink and blue were first introduced after World War I as colors to differentiate boy and girl infants, pink was the boy's color because pink was "stronger" and blue was "delicate" and therefore suitable for girls.[36] In the 1940s the color preferences switched partly due to retail marketing.[37] Today many think of these color associations as absolute, but in reality they are not even a century old.

Another problem with essentialist thinking is that it fails to recognize how gender training is deeply embedded in all aspects of society. Family, school, friends, church, movies, television, and social media all abound with messages about what is suitable for males and females. Cultures have shaming words for both males and females who seem to depart from the expected norms. There is intense social pressure on both males and females to conform to social expectations.[38]

Third, essentialist thinking fails to take into account individual and personality differences. Instead, it labels certain personality traits and behaviors as inherently masculine and others as inherently feminine. Women are associated with gentleness, kindness, and patience, for example, while men are associated with strength and firmness. Yet large-scale research shows that there are no significant personality differences between men and women. In other words, most people are a blend of characteristics stereotypically attributed to men and to women. The researchers conclude, "If you try to guess someone's personality from their gender, you'll very often be wrong."[39]

Why do the ideas of separate spheres and gender essentialism matter? Miller and Borgida explain how separate spheres

36. Maglaty, "When Did Girls Start Wearing Pink?"
37. Maglaty, "When Did Girls Start Wearing Pink?"
38. Dzubinski and Diehl, "Problem of Gender Essentialism," 57.
39. Spencer Greenberg and Holly Muir, "Most of Us Combine Personality Traits from Different Genders," *Scientific American*, January 31, 2022, https://www.scientificamerican.com/article/most-of-us-combine-personality-traits-from-different-genders/.

ideology "harms both men and women (although not necessarily in directly comparable ways) by restricting women's abilities to contribute fully to society and restricting men's abilities to participate fully in their family lives."[40] In their extensive research with over thirteen hundred participants, they learned that stronger beliefs in separate spheres for men and women led employees to resist workplace flexibility practices that would help both women and men better care for their families and that would help women contribute more economically to their families. Such beliefs even led to more discrimination by managers against women employees.[41] Separate spheres thinking and gender essentialist thinking lead to the kinds of gendered assumptions and stereotypical statements that opened this chapter.

The Two-Person Career

One more challenge for many Christian organizations is an unspoken assumption that if a married man is hired for a role, his wife will voluntarily contribute her time and energy to the work as well. This expectation is called the two-person career structure and was first named by Hanna Papanek in the 1970s. Papanek explains that the two-person career is "a special combination of roles which I call the 'two-person single career.' This combination of formal and informal institutional demands . . . is placed on both members of a married couple of whom

40. Miller and Borgida, "Separate Spheres Model," 4.
41. Miller and Borgida, "Separate Spheres Model," 28–30. Interestingly, the discrimination was reported by the managers themselves, against women as well as against men who wanted flexibility to engage in family caretaking. They reported engaging in behaviors such as reconsidering a promotion, terminating the employee, asking the employee to quit, preventing the employee from having time off or changing their schedule, demoting the employee, and cutting the employee's hours. The more strongly the manager endorsed the belief that women belong at home and men at work, the more likely they were to engage in these discriminatory behaviors.

only the man is employed by the institution."[42] Papanek further explains, "The 'two-person career' pattern is fully congruent with the stereotype of the wife as supporter, comforter, back-stage manager, home maintainer, and main rearer of children."[43] Note that the two-person career expectation is built on an assumption of separate spheres.

Papanek initially named the military, high-level politicians, ambassadors, and university professors as functioning in a two-person career. Other researchers soon pointed out that clergy and missionary are other clear examples of a two-person career expectation.[44] It is also worth noting that the expectation rarely works in reverse. If a married woman is hired into a role, organizations are unlikely to expect her husband's voluntary contributions. Finally, the expectation is not always explicit. Sometimes both members of a couple are interviewed even if only one is being hired, though that approach is typically illegal. Other times, the expectations are simply present, unspoken, and taken for granted. An employee may not know the expectation even exists until it crops up after hiring.

A two-person career expectation presents several challenges for women. First is the extra work. If she has her own career and is expected to contribute to her husband's work as well, that can be a heavy load. Second is the unpaid nature of two-person career work. While the man is hired and paid for his contributions, the woman's contributions are not seen as valuable enough to be compensated. She is not an organizational employee. That the work is not paid may be why the role only

---

42. Hanna Papanek, "Men, Women, and Work: Reflections on the Two-Person Career," *The American Journal of Sociology* 78, no. 4 (1973): 852.

43. Papanek, "Men, Women, and Work," 853.

44. Gail Murphy-Geiss, "Married to the Minister: The Status of the Clergy Spouse as Part of a Two-Person Single Career," *Journal of Family Issues* 32, no. 7 (2011): 932; Marsha Wiggins Frame and Constance L. Shehan, "Work and Well-Being in the Two-Person Career: Relocation Stress and Coping Among Clergy Husbands and Wives," *Family Relations*, no. 2 (1994): 196.

works one way: Men's time is seen as inherently more valuable than women's and therefore not expected to be donated for free.

Putting all this together, American society has a system in which the following assumptions operate: First, the ideal worker is a male with someone taking care of all personal needs. Second, the organization is greedy, demanding total loyalty to the cause. Third, men are believed to belong in the workplace, and women are believed to belong in the domestic sphere. Fourth, essentialist thinking reinforces the belief in separate spheres since women are deemed "fit" for the domestic sphere and men "fit" for the public sphere. Last, married men are assumed to have wives who will not only take care of all personal needs but also voluntarily contribute time and energy to the man's employer. This combination of assumptions leads to a dynamic where women feel they can never get it right. They cannot be an ideal worker; they cannot fulfill the demands of two greedy institutions (work and family), although the psychological and social expectations are that they should. Women's suitability for the workplace in the first place is doubted, and they do not come with a spouse-volunteer to help them meet the demands of the organization. Women are left feeling exhausted, hopeless, and like they can never get it right. And in this system, they are correct: They cannot get it all right.

Resisting the Ideal Worker Mythology

Up until the COVID-19 pandemic that started in March 2020, not many people outside of academia questioned the "ideal worker" and "greedy institution" paradigms that make up so much of American society. Everyone simply accepted that model of how work is done. But the global pandemic shook up the world of work and made many people question how they work, when they work, and how work gets done. Suddenly it became clear that many jobs could be done remotely and with flexibility. And of course the pandemic shed more light on the double burden of work and family that has always been shouldered by women.[45]

The stress caused by the pandemic brought a number of new terms into US vocabulary to describe worker exhaustion: "the great resignation," "quiet quitting," the "great gloom," and the "great detachment," among others.[46] What COVID made clear was that the dominant paradigms for work were not actually working well for many individuals and families. Consider the definition of "quiet quitting." Quiet quitting has been described as "not answering emails or phone calls outside of work hours, saying no to new projects not part of a worker's job description . . . and leaving work on time every day."[47] In fact this definition of quiet quitting describes someone not willing to perform the "ideal worker" role any longer, opting instead to do the job without going above and beyond all the time. Yet somehow rather than being seen as a reasonable choice, such behavior has now been labeled "quitting," as if by not doing excess, the employee is not doing the job at all. Something is terribly wrong with that idea.

45. Chantal Remery et al., "Gender and Employment: Recalibrating Women's Position in Work, Organizations, and Society in Times of COVID-19," *Gender, Work & Organization* 29, no. 6 (2022): 1927; John Bluedorn et al., "Gender and Employment in the COVID-19 Recession: Cross-Country Evidence on 'She-Cessions,'" *Labour Economics* 81 (2023): 1–10.

46. For data on the great resignation, see Vincent Amanor-Boadu, "Empirical Evidence for the 'Great Resignation,'" *Monthly Labor Review*, U.S. Bureau of Labor Statistics, November 2022, https://www.bls.gov/opub/mlr/2022/article/empirical-evidence-for-the-great-resignation.htm. For more on "quiet quitting," see Tingting Zhang and Chloe Rodrigue, "What If Moms Quiet Quit? The Role of Maternity Leave Policy in Working Mothers' Quiet Quitting Behaviors," *Merits* 3, no. 1 (2023): 186–205. For more on the "great gloom," see "The Great Gloom: In 2023, Employees Are Unhappier Than Ever," Bamboo HR, 2023, https://www.bamboohr.com/resources/guides/employee-happiness-h1-2023. For more on the "great detachment," see Kimberly Bond, "Feeling Despondent at Work? Why 2025 Is Set to Be the Year of the 'Great Detachment,'" *Bazaar*, April 16, 2025, https://www.harpersbazaar.com/culture/a64502127/great-detachment-career-trend/.

47. Zhang and Rodrigue, "What If Moms Quiet Quit?," 186.

Scripture's Perspective

Let's take a look at what the Bible has to say about these societal ideas of ideal workers, greedy institutions, separate spheres, two-person career expectations, and gender essentialist thinking. What does it have to say about the role of work and family in Christian life? Is it true that the Bible expects women to remain primarily in the domestic sphere, and that it expects men and women to exhibit different, opposite characteristics as good Christians?

Created for Meaningful Work

The creation narrative in Genesis 1 shows that both humans, male and female, were created for and expected to do meaningful work. Men and women are given the same instructions: Both are expected to work the garden and to procreate. Genesis 1:28 says, "God blessed them, and God said to them, 'Be fruitful and multiply and fill the earth and subdue it and have dominion over the fish of the sea and over the birds of the air and over every living thing that moves upon the earth.'" According to Philip Payne, "God gives both man and woman the same blessing and the same dominion over the earth and all the animals. Their equality is evident in the thirteen words that are plural in Hebrew [in Gen. 1:28], including Hebrew verbs that specify a plural subject."[48] He concludes, "Genesis 1 does not teach any difference between the responsibilities or roles of men and women."[49]

Interestingly, a poor translation of 1 Timothy 5:8 taken out of context is sometimes used as an argument that men are the ones primarily responsible to provide financially for their families. The ESV says, "But if anyone does not provide for his

---

48. Philip Barton Payne, *The Bible vs. Biblical Womanhood: How God's Word Consistently Affirms Gender Equality* (Zondervan, 2023), 1.
49. Payne, *The Bible vs. Biblical Womanhood*, 2.

relatives, and especially for members of his household, he has denied the faith and is worse than an unbeliever."[50] However, that is not an appropriate reading of the passage in its context; rather, the verse has been lifted out and used as a proof-text for men to be a family's primary breadwinner.

In the context of 1 Timothy 5, Paul is giving instructions to Timothy for specific groups of leaders in the church. Paul writes, "Do not speak harshly to an older man, but speak to him as to a father, to younger men as brothers, to older women as mothers, to younger women as sisters—with absolute purity" (5:1–2).[51] According to Payne, the formula of older men, older women, younger men, younger women that Paul uses in Titus 2 and also here in 1 Timothy 5 is meant for experienced and novice elders in the church, both men and women elders, not older and younger people.[52] That understanding fits with the next group Paul addresses in this text, widows, who constituted an office of service in the early church.[53] In verses 3–7 Paul explains how they should carry out their duties. Then, finally, comes verse 8. In the context, coming after instructions regarding elders and widows, Paul does not suddenly turn his attention to individual men. Instead, he is discussing all the church leaders he has just named—that is why he uses the pronoun "anyone."

The verse itself contains no male pronouns.[54] Nevertheless, a few Bible translations say, "if any man" rather than "if anyone."[55] Worse, practically every English translation adds male pronouns

---

50. Functional-equivalence translations make it clear that the verse is not directed only to males.

51. This verse is an example of how insisting on a formal-equivalence translation actually obscures the meaning of the original author.

52. Payne, *The Bible vs. Biblical Womanhood*, 161–68.

53. Leanne M. Dzubinski and Anneke H. Stasson, *Women in the Mission of the Church: Their Opportunities and Obstacles Throughout Christian History* (Baker Academic, 2021), 23–27.

54. The Greek pronoun *tis* is correctly translated as "anyone."

55. Phillips, Wycliffe, and the Worldwide English Translation all use "man" for the pronoun "anyone."

like "he" and "his" to the English text—pronouns that are not in the Greek text.[56] These changes and additions to the verse mistakenly give the impression that men are in view with the instructions. But that does not work logically, given the context, or grammatically, given the wording of the original text. The instructions are for church leaders and parallel the requirements in 1 Timothy 3 that church leaders manage their own households well.[57]

Similarly to the mistaken use of 1 Timothy 5:8, a Bible passage that is sometimes used to argue that women belong only in the home is Titus 2:4–5. The passage says, "Instruct the younger women in good judgment: to love their husbands and children, to be self-controlled, pure, good household managers, kind, submitting to their own husbands so that no one will malign the word of God."[58] Read through a twenty-first-century lens, these verses seem to tell women to stay home, and indeed many English translations use phrases like "working at home" (ESV), "keepers at home" (KJV), "spending their time in their own homes" (The Living Bible), "workers at home" (NASB), "busy at home" (NIV), and even "good housewives" (Good News Translation). The problem with all these modern translations is that they have used today's language to describe the first century. Remember, prior to the industrial revolution, there was little separation of home and work. Factories and offices did not exist. A woman who worked at home or managed the home was working in the family business. So a woman who is a

56. For example, ASV, ESV, NASB, NASB95, NET, NKJV, RSV, and Young's Literal translation all use "he" and "his family" in 1 Tim. 5:8.

57. See verses 4 and 12. A discussion of elders is beyond the scope of this book, but Payne makes similar arguments about that passage, and the addition of male pronouns in English translations that are not present in Greek is similarly problematic.

58. Translation from Payne, *The Bible vs. Biblical Womanhood*, 161. The NRSV also uses "good managers of the household" as the translation; the International Standard Version, the Tree of Life translation and the VOICE translation also use forms of "manage."

"good manager of the household" is effectively a good manager of the family business.

Finally, it is also problematic to use such verses and a pre–industrial revolution family structure as a basis for expecting married women today to serve as unpaid volunteers for their husband's workplace. Old Testament law specifically forbids withholding a worker's wages.[59] When Jesus is sending out the seventy-two disciples in Luke 10, he states that "the laborer deserves to be paid" (v. 7). Similar instructions are repeated in Matthew 10:10 and 1 Timothy 5:18. How ironic that women who minister alongside their husbands today are often expected to do so in unpaid roles, in direct contradiction to biblical teaching.

Women as Managers

In 2004 Ann Crittenden published a book called *If You've Raised Kids, You Can Manage Anything.* Her book describes the multitude of ways managing a home, raising children, and keeping things running smoothly for the family requires exactly the same types of managerial skills that are needed in many workplaces. The Bible, too, offers several examples of women who are good managers and who manage large family businesses.

THE PROVERBS 31 WOMAN

Contrary to some popular Bible teaching, the woman of Proverbs 31 is not an example of a modern-day housewife. Rather, she is managing a household economy that includes making cloth, planting a vineyard (which presumably included harvesting the grapes and making wine), overseeing workers, trading her goods with other merchants, selling her wares to others, and teaching. Today she would be called an entrepreneur

---

59. See Lev. 19:13 and Deut. 24:15.

or a small business owner. Her work may be based out of the home (as virtually all work was prior to the industrial revolution), but she is not solely focused on what constitutes housework in the twenty-first century.[60]

ABIGAIL

Abigail is another example of an Old Testament woman with many responsibilities. Her story is told in 1 Samuel 25:2–42. She was the wife of a wealthy Calebite man named Nabal. The narrator says that she was "intelligent and beautiful," but that Nabal was "surly and mean in his dealings" (25:3 NIV). As the story continues, Nabal's stingy attitude becomes clear when he refuses to perform the expected hospitality of his day for David and David's men who had been protecting Nabal's shepherds and flocks for months. Even Nabal's servants know his shortcomings, but perhaps Abigail as the household manager knows them best. After all, when Nabal responds with hostility to David's culturally appropriate request for provisions, one of the servants goes to Abigail for help. Clearly she has oversight of the household stores and provisions, for she immediately assembles a large gift for David and his men: "two hundred loaves, two skins of wine, five sheep ready dressed, five measures of parched grain, one hundred clusters of raisins, and two hundred cakes of figs" (25:18). She also has agency, because she loads the provision on the donkeys and goes along behind the servants to meet David's men. Finally, she has spiritual knowledge because she knows that David has been chosen by God to rule.[61] She believes it and acts out of that belief. The examples of these women show that women are created for

60. In no way do I diminish the work of housewives. Housework is clearly real work and when done in practically any setting other than the home, it is remunerated. It is the setting of the home that requires free, unpaid labor, not the work itself that is somehow less valuable.
61. She says to David, "When the LORD has fulfilled for my lord every good thing he promised concerning him and has appointed him ruler over Israel . . ." (1 Sam.

and able to work productively for the good of their families and their societies.

Characteristics of Women and Men

As previously discussed, research does not support the idea that men and women are somehow fundamentally different. Nor can the idea that men are expected to exhibit one set of characteristics and women another be supported from the Bible. Scripture makes abundantly clear that women and men are saved in the same way, gifted with the same gifts by the same Holy Spirit, and held to the same criteria for godly behavior. In short there are no gendered lists of gifts, virtues, or sins to be found.

SPIRITUAL GIFTS

Both 1 Corinthians and Romans discuss the gifts given by the Holy Spirit to followers of Jesus for the good of the church. Paul starts his explanation to the Corinthian believers with this statement: "Now concerning spiritual gifts, brothers and sisters, I do not want you to be ignorant" (1 Cor. 12:1). Instead, he wants them to be informed, so he explains how spiritual gifts work:

> Now there are varieties of gifts but the same Spirit, and there are varieties of services but the same Lord, and there are varieties of activities, but it is the same God who activates all of them in everyone. To each is given the manifestation of the Spirit for the common good. To one is given through the Spirit the utterance of wisdom and to another the utterance of knowledge according to the same Spirit, to another faith by the same Spirit, to another gifts of healing by the one Spirit, to another the working of powerful deeds, to another prophecy, to another the

---

25:30 NIV). The story does not tell us how she knows this information, but it is clear that she knows and believes.

discernment of spirits, to another various kinds of tongues, to another the interpretation of tongues. All these are activated by one and the same Spirit, who allots to each one individually just as the Spirit chooses. (12:4–11)

There is no trace of gendered language here, no suggestion that some gifts are for men and others for women. In fact, in his letter to the Romans, Paul does explain how different gifts are apportioned, and it is not based on gender: "We have gifts that differ according to the grace given to us: prophecy, in proportion to faith; ministry, in ministering; the teacher, in teaching; the encourager, in encouragement; the giver, in sincerity; the leader, in diligence; the compassionate, in cheerfulness" (Rom 12:6–8). The basis for different gifts is God's grace, not human gender.

VIRTUES AND VICES

Furthermore, there are no virtue lists or sin lists that are differentiated based on gender. Instead, scriptural messages are addressed to all believers. For example, Paul writes this to the Ephesian believers:

I, therefore, the prisoner in the Lord, beg you to walk in a manner worthy of the calling to which you have been called, with all humility and gentleness, with patience, bearing with one another in love, making every effort to maintain the unity of the Spirit in the bond of peace: there is one body and one Spirit, just as you were called to the one hope of your calling, one Lord, one faith, one baptism, one God and Father of all, who is above all and through all and in all. (4:1–6)

He appeals to Christian unity in the faith, not separating or dividing people by gender, role, or any other human distinction.

Similarly, when Paul writes about bad behavior, there is no division based on gender. Sin is sin, whether committed by a man or a woman. Paul explains, "Now the works of the flesh are obvious: sexual immorality, impurity, debauchery, idolatry, sorcery, enmities, strife, jealousy, anger, quarrels, dissensions, factions, envy, drunkenness, carousing, and things like these. I am warning you, as I warned you before: those who do such things will not inherit the kingdom of God" (Gal. 5:19–21). In short there is no scriptural support to assign some characteristics to men and others to women. Such ideas come from society, not the Bible, and have no place among Jesus's followers.

COMMANDS FOR REST AND SABBATH

Finally, the concepts of rest and Sabbath are also clearly taught in the Bible. The fourth commandment teaches the Israelites to "observe the Sabbath day and keep it holy" (Deut. 5:12). Moses reminded them that not keeping the Sabbath rest was a capital crime.[62] Other Old Testament passages reinforced the importance of Sabbath, and various prophets chastised the Israelites when they failed to keep the Sabbath (see Neh. 13:15–18; Isa. 58:13–14; Jer. 17:21–23; Ezek. 20:11–13, 24). By the time of Jesus, the Sabbath had become in some ways legalistic, and Jesus criticized the Pharisees for using it for their own purposes (e.g., Matt. 12:1–8). Yet Jesus clearly still practiced and encouraged his disciples to withdraw from ministry for times of rest and rejuvenation. Luke 5:16 describes his practice: "He would slip away to deserted places and pray." Or consider Matthew 14:13: When Jesus learned of the death of his cousin John, he withdrew and took time to grieve. Such practices are countercultural in some circles of American society, yet rest is a critical need for humans to flourish. Scripture does not glorify overwork; rather it encourages Christians to rest and worship.

62. "Six days shall work be done, but on the seventh day you shall have a holy Sabbath of solemn rest to the Lord; whoever does any work on it shall be put to death" (Exod. 35:2).

Strategies to Thrive as Whole People

Organizational strategies for helping employees and organizational members to thrive as whole people are both straightforward and complex. The ideas are not particularly difficult, yet it may require diligence to change workplace cultures of overwork and mistaken gender essentialist views that make it harder for women to thrive. On the simple side are building in workplace flexibility and setting boundaries around work expectations. On the more challenging side is changing ingrained thinking about gender and priorities. First I will look at the concrete steps, then I will offer some thoughts on changing organizational culture.

Implement Workplace Flexibility

The solutions to quitting, gloom, detachment, and a host of other workplace ills are clear. Study after study shows that employees prize flexibility above pretty much every other workplace benefit. The Conference Board found that 65 percent of workers listed workplace flexibility as the benefit they most valued.[63] Similarly, Bankrate found that fully 89 percent of employees support some form of flexibility, including a four-day workweek, hybrid work, or remote work.[64] Both of these surveys also found that women and younger workers have particularly strong preferences for flexible work arrangements. The gender and generational differences are not huge, but they are noticeable. As the Bankrate study noted, "Though shorter workweeks, hybrid work and remote work are widely popular, they're especially popular among young and female full-time

---

63. "Survey: US Employees Prioritize Workplace Flexibility as a Key Component of Compensation," The Conference Board, November 7, 2023, https://www.conference-board.org/press/workplace-flexibility?tpcc=NL_Marketing.

64. Lane G. Gillespie, "Survey: 89% of American Workforce Prefer 4-Day Workweeks, Remote Work or Hybrid Work," Bankrate, August 23, 2023, https://www.bankrate.com/personal-finance/hybrid-remote-and-4-day-workweek-survey/.

workers."[65] Because of the attractiveness of flexible work, the Conference Board report concludes, "Firms that don't offer flexible options will face an increasingly limited hiring pool" of employees.[66]

Hybrid work, which is defined as some days in the office and some working from home, seems to be a particularly good choice for employee productivity and well-being. Managers worry that hybrid workers are less productive, but research does not support their concerns. In a report presented by the Stanford Institute for Economic Policy Research, Jose Barrero, Nicholas Bloom, and Stephen Davis analyzed multiple studies of worker productivity and well-being. They concluded, "These studies suggest that working from home one or two days a week improves productivity and leads to happier employees."[67]

Of course not all types of work can be done remotely. Churches and many other Christian institutions would fall into Barrero, Bloom, and Davis's category of "Professional and Business Services" and Christian colleges and universities would fall into their "Education" category. Both types of organizations, post-pandemic, typically already offer some flexibility. For example, teachers and professors may need to be on-site for classes but can prepare lessons and grade remotely. Clergy may preach and conduct Bible studies in person but can study and prepare remotely. Nonprofits like mission agencies and social service agencies are also well-suited to flexible work arrangements, with some events and social services that require on-site attendance while other responsibilities may be carried out remotely.

Additionally, all of these institutions are to some degree "greedy." The work and ministry demands are seemingly endless; work does not fit neatly into a five-day, forty-hour work

65. Gillespie, "Survey."
66. "Survey: US Employees."
67. Jose Maria Barrero, Nicholas Bloom, and Stephen J. Davis, "The Evolution of Work from Home," *Journal of Economic Perspectives* 37, no. 4 (2023): 21.

week. Boundaries are porous with evening and weekend responsibilities being the norm for many. To prevent burnout, promote work well-being, and achieve their mission and goals, Christian organizations would do well on a practical level to promote flexible schedules with hybrid and remote options for many of their employees. Leaders should help members of the organization to set, and keep, reasonable boundaries around work.

Revising job descriptions is another effective strategy to support flourishing. Ensure job expectations are realistic for both men and women. Make sure there are no hidden expectations of unpaid volunteer work from an employee's spouse: No job should require the work of two people for completion. Work is not the sum total of a person's life. Make sure employees have space for family, friends, rest, exercise, hobbies, and other activities.

Change Ingrained Thinking: Leaders Model the Way

For effective organizational change to occur, it is imperative that leaders model the way. In practical terms, that means leaders need to use flexible schedules as appropriate, go home at reasonable hours, take their vacations, send email only during work hours, and generally show by example that it is okay for people to set boundaries around their work. Leaders must clearly communicate and show that flexibility and boundaries will not be stigmatized or viewed as less than full commitment.

Leaders also need to be first to challenge essentialist statements. Any comment that generalizes characteristics of men or women is likely an essentialist statement and is probably off-putting to some listeners, both men and women. If you hear someone say that men or women are "naturally" something, be the first to question that assumption. In the same way, leaders can learn to recognize and challenge separate spheres thinking. Comments about "women's place" or "men's responsibility" reflect poor theology and need to be corrected with good theological thinking.

Leaders are also the ones who need to combat greedy institution thinking. No organization or institution should be the highest priority in a person's life. Yet the demands of greedy institutions can create cultures of loyalty, where the good of the institution is seen as the highest value. Such an attitude is a kind of idolatry, where God and God's kingdom are replaced with human institutions. People are eternal; organizations are not. Yet far too often the values driving an organization are reversed, as if the people exist to serve the institution rather than the institution existing to serve people. Leaders must learn to see such beliefs and work to combat them. When people flourish, the organization will flourish.

This kind of work to change ingrained thinking and default attitudes is difficult. Often people do not even realize they hold such beliefs, or they have never been offered any alternative way of viewing others or viewing work. It is the old adage about the fish not being able to see its own water. The leader's job is to make the water visible. When something can be seen, it can be changed. When problems have names, they can be addressed and solved. As long as they remain invisible, they will dominate, regardless of whether they are healthy or desirable. Leaders do the hard work of making problems visible and creating conditions for change.

Chapter Summary

This chapter has looked at a constellation of attitudes and beliefs that make it challenging for women to thrive in an organization. Greedy institutions demand total commitment, and both ministry organizations and families are characterized as greedy. Women can never adequately fulfill either set of demands, let alone both. Next is the trifecta of separate spheres thinking, gender essentialist beliefs, and two-person career expectations, which together create cultures where women are not seen as fully belonging in the workplace. These ideas portray women as belonging in the home and supporting a husband's career. Yet these beliefs have come from culture, not the Bible, and do not accurately reflect God's design for human flourishing. Christian organizations need to do careful work to examine their unspoken beliefs and theologies. Once these faulty ways of thinking have been identified, practical steps can be taken to change organizational cultures into spaces where everyone—women and men—can thrive in their callings.

4

"Are You Sure That's Right?"

Ambivalence Toward Women

Male executives called one nonprofit leader "sweetie," "dear," and "hon." She explained, "They are meaning it in a nice way, like they see me like a granddaughter, but it comes off condescending and somewhat demeaning because I'm not a child and this is a professional setting."

—nonprofit leader[1]

Instead of saying, "Oh, I'm sure she and HR have really good reasons; maybe we should talk about it with her," the leader sided with the employee and all of a sudden I had zero authority.

—mission leader[2]

1. Amy B. Diehl and Leanne M. Dzubinski, "We Need to Talk About Using Pet Names for Women at Work," *Fast Company*, October 29, 2020, https://www.fastcompany.com/90569439/we-need-to-talk-about-using-pet-names-for-women-at-work.
2. This quotation was collected as part of my own research that has not yet been published and is quoted by permission of the interviewee.

A consistent problem that women encounter at work is ambivalence toward them and their presence.[3] It is a problem that shows up in many different ways, from subtle to overt. The opening stories are just two examples. In the first, men in the organization refer to a woman—who is younger than them—with pet names.[4] As she notes, by treating her as a granddaughter and talking to her as if they were at home, not at work, they are not taking her seriously as a colleague. Looking down on women because of their age—any age—and talking to them as if the setting were home instead of work communicates to women that they are less valued and less welcome in the workplace than men.[5]

In the second scenario, the woman did her job, but her subordinate complained to her supervisor. The supervisor overturned the decision without even talking to her. After it happened, she realized that what she said did not matter, and the people she supervised stopped taking her seriously. She felt—and had been—undercut in her work. Such lack of support comes from ambivalence toward women's presence in the Christian workplace.

There are many other ways women find themselves treated with ambivalence. Pet names and diminutives suggest that women really belong in the home, not at work. Leaving off women's titles when men's titles are being used reduces women's perceived authority. Credibility deficit happens when people—usually men—do not believe what women say. Lack of support

---

3. See Leanne M. Dzubinski, *Playing by the Rules: How Women Lead in Evangelical Mission Organizations*, American Society of Missiology Monograph Series 52 (Pickwick, 2021), for a fuller discussion of ambivalence.

4. Diehl and Dzubinski, "We Need to Talk About Using Pet Names for Women at Work."

5. For more on how gendered ageism functions in the workplace, see Amy B. Diehl, Leanne M. Dzubinski, and Amber L. Stephenson, "Women in Leadership Face Ageism at Every Age," *Harvard Business Review*, June 16, 2023, https://hbr.org/2023/06/women-in-leadership-face-ageism-at-every-age.

when women do their jobs undermines their confidence. Underpaying or not paying women communicates that their contributions are less valuable than those of their male counterparts. All these actions likely stem from sexist attitudes toward women. Sexism can be hostile, or it can be benevolent or even sanctified.[6] Benevolent and sanctified sexism may look kind on the surface, but such attitudes function to undermine women's agency. All of these behaviors are subtle and not-so-subtle ways that organizations and leaders communicate to women that they might not really belong at work. And all of them need to be addressed to create a healthy working environment for everyone. In this chapter I will look at these problems, consider what God has to say about women, and review strategies to eliminate these damaging practices.

Ways Women are Treated with Ambivalence

For much of history, it was simply accepted that women were less valuable and less important than men. Aristotle thought men were superior to women; his thinking influenced the entire world into which the church was born and heavily influenced early church thinkers.[7] Because of Aristotle, "a strand of thought that depicted women as in some ways inferior to men was woven in" to the early church.[8] Medieval teachers picked up on it, as did some Reformers, and their teaching continues to impact the church to the present day. However, in the mid-twentieth century, thanks in part to the second-wave

---

6. For more on this, see the "Sanctified Sexism" section below.

7. Alice P. Mathews, *Gender Roles and the People of God: Rethinking What We Were Taught About Men and Women in the Church* (Zondervan, 2017); Heather Matthews, *Confronting Sexism in the Church: How We Got Here and What We Can Do About It* (IVP, 2024), 51.

8. Leanne M. Dzubinski and Anneke H. Stasson, *Women in the Mission of the Church: Their Opportunities and Obstacles Throughout Christian History* (Baker Academic, 2021), 2–3.

women's rights movements and better biblical scholarship, many organizations and churches started to move away from such overt forms of sexist thinking. As women gained access to education, voting, bank accounts, and employment, they began to be viewed as equals with men.[9] Unfortunately, that did not mean that attitudes changed or that discrimination against women disappeared. Instead, bias and discrimination continue, sometimes in overt ways and often in more subtle ones, leading to the problem of ambivalence.[10] In this section I name and describe eight specific attitudes and practices that are common in Christian organizations and that communicate ambivalence to women.

Pet Names

As described in the opening quotations, one particularly frustrating issue that women encounter routinely in the workplace is being referred to with pet names and diminutives. The opening scenario in this chapter is the commentary of a woman working for a Christian nonprofit. Terms like "honey," "sweetie," "dear," and "girl" may be appropriate for the home setting and close familial relationships, but they do not belong in the workplace. At work they are inappropriate and sometimes demeaning. The subtle message of such pet names is that women belong at home, not at work. Christian workplaces are not the only ones with this problem; in my research, women from all kinds of fields and industries talked about this

9. When we moved to Austria in 1995, I could not get a safety deposit box at the bank without my husband's signature. In Spain under Franco (1892–1975) women could not get bank accounts or driver's licenses, among other things, without their husband's permission. See Celia Valiente, "Age and Feminist Activism: The Feminist Protest Within the Catholic Church in Franco's Spain," *Social Movement Studies* 14, no. 4 (2015): 490.

10. Amber L. Stephenson et al., *An Exploration of Gender Bias Affecting Women in Medicine*, The Contributions of Health Care Management to Grand Health Care Challenges 20 (Emerald, 2021), 78.

problem.[11] However, since many Christian organizations think of and talk about themselves in family terms, such language may not be recognized as problematic until someone points it out.

Not Using Titles

Another way of communicating ambivalence to women is failing to use their professional titles when appropriate. Instead, women are addressed by their first name or a marital status such as "Ms." or "Mrs." Marital titles focus on women's relationship to men, not their professional qualifications. Or their qualifications are omitted in written material when men's qualifications are used. The problem is so pervasive that my colleague and I created words for it: "untitling" and "uncredentialing."[12] We wanted women to have a name for this action and be able to recognize it as a form of gender bias. Over the years as a professor in Christian institutions, I have observed with interest which students call me by my title and which ones assume they can use my first name. Frequently it is white male students who will call me by my first name without an invitation to do so. Women and students of color tend to be more respectful of titles. I am not alone in noticing this trend; studies show that women faculty are more likely to have their titles omitted than are men; so are women physicians.[13] Women clergy report the same problem,

---

11. Diehl and Dzubinski, "We Need to Talk About Using Pet Names for Women at Work."

12. Amy B. Diehl and Leanne M. Dzubinski, "We Need to Stop 'Untitling' and 'Uncredentialing' Professional Women," *Fast Company*, January 22, 2021, https:// www.fastcompany.com/90596628/we-need-to-stop-untitling-and-uncredentialing -professional-women.

13. Amy B. Diehl and Leanne M. Dzubinski, *Glass Walls: Shattering the Six Gender Bias Barriers That Still Hold Women Back at Work* (Rowman & Littlefield, 2023), 101; Susan K. Pingleton et al., "Silent Bias: Challenges, Obstacles, and Strategies for Leadership Development in Academic Medicine—Lessons From Oral Histories of Women Professors at the University of Kansas," *Academic Medicine* 91, no. 8 (2016): 1153; Whitney H. Sherman et al., "Unwritten: Young

as do women in many other professions that include titles, such as coaches and military personnel.[14] Not using women's professional titles when men's titles are being used is another way of communicating ambivalence toward women's presence. Focusing on marital status instead of professional title signals that women belong at home, not in the workplace. Omitted titles can be especially galling if a pet name is used instead, relegating the woman to the status of a child.

Credibility Deficit

If you have ever heard the question, "Are you sure that's right?" posed to a woman who stated something, you have seen credibility deficit in action. Or perhaps you saw a male listener turn to the nearest male to ask if what a woman just said was correct. Credibility deficit occurs when listeners do not believe what a woman says.[15] It has happened to me numerous times. Once at church, I explained to the elders that their way of calculating votes was mathematically incorrect. They disagreed; only months later did someone review the math and realize I had been correct. Another time it happened on a retreat. A man asked me about a topic in my area of expertise, and after I answered his question he turned to my husband and asked if what I had said was correct. The man who asked the question may not remember the event, but I still do. I wondered why he had even bothered to ask me if he did not think my answer would be trustworthy. My experiences are not unique; women in my research report being doubted in all kinds of settings.

People have been distrusting women's accounts of events forever. In 2007, Dr. Miranda Fricker named this tendency to

---

Women Faculty in Educational Leadership," *Journal of Educational Administration* 48, no. 6 (2010): 745.

14. Diehl and Dzubinski, "We Need to Stop 'Untitling' and 'Uncredentialing' Professional Women."

15. Diehl and Dzubinski, *Glass Walls*, 117.

disbelieve women's accounts of events "testimonial injustice."[16] Women know they may not be believed, which partly explains their reluctance to report domestic violence, sexual harassment, and sexual assault.[17] Women may decide, quite reasonably, that going through the stress of reporting such incidents is not worth the pain involved, given the likelihood that they will not be believed or that they may experience backlash for reporting bad behavior.[18] Those cases may be extreme, yet even when talking about less somber issues, not having one's expertise taken seriously at work is highly frustrating and detracts from women's ability to do their job. Instead they have to invest time and energy defending their role and their expertise, time that could be better spent fulfilling their responsibilities.

Lack of Support

Many women in Christian organizations describe not being given the necessary support to do their jobs properly. Lack of support in Christian workplaces can show up in a variety of ways. It can mean lack of funding or other necessary resources. It can mean lack of authority to carry out their responsibilities. A particularly frustrating way organizations show lack of support is by assigning a woman an interim role. One mission leader explained, "I knew if I did this as an interim, there was a risk that I could lose everything. They could say, well, we don't want to keep you on full-time, and by that time be too late to go back to my other position; they would have replaced me by then."[19] The organization expected her to take all the risk, while offering her no guarantee of support. Another leader

---

16. Miranda Fricker, *Epistemic Injustice: Power and the Ethics of Knowing* (Oxford University Press, 2007).

17. Heather Stewart, "'Why Didn't She Say Something Sooner?': Doubt, Denial, Silencing, and the Epistemic Harms of the #MeToo Movement," *South Central Review* 36, no. 2 (2019): 84–85.

18. Diehl and Dzubinski, *Glass Walls*, 142–43.

19. Dzubinski, *Playing by the Rules*, 134.

described, "When they said I had to be the interim for a year I didn't like that. I thought, if you believe in me, or if you think I'm qualified for this job, hire me!"[20] She clearly perceived the interim assignment as signaling lack of support for her leadership role. The interim role communicates that the woman must prove herself before she can be considered for the permanent role. And frequently, after taking the interim position, she is then passed over for the permanent one.

Lack of support can also show up in more active ways through undermining, such as overturning decisions or taking a man's side in a disagreement without ever hearing the woman's perspective on events, as the second opening illustration showed.[21] Each of these events communicates to the woman that while she may be tolerated in the workplace, she does not fully belong. In effect, the organizational leaders making these decisions are showing ambivalence to her presence.[22]

Missing in Leadership Roles

Yet another way that Christian organizations communicate ambivalence toward women is by not having them in positions of organizational leadership, particularly positions at the top. In their three-phase study of Christian organizations, researchers Janel Curry and Amy Reynolds surveyed and then interviewed people in hundreds of organizations to see how women fared in leadership roles. They found that 25 percent of organizations had no women at all on their board of directors.[23]

20. Dzubinski, *Playing by the Rules*, 172.

21. Amy B. Diehl and Leanne M. Dzubinski, "Making the Invisible Visible: A Cross-Sector Analysis of Gender-Based Leadership Barriers," *Human Resource Development Quarterly* 27, no. 2 (2016): 189–90; Dzubinski, *Playing by the Rules*, 175–83.

22. Dzubinski, *Playing by the Rules*, 167–80.

23. Janel Curry and Amy Reynolds, *Missional Effectiveness: Achieving Institutional Goals and Mission*, Women in Leadership National Study (Gordon College, 2017), 4.

Women in CEO and board leadership roles were more prevalent in organizations with smaller budgets and fewer personnel.[24] The researchers also noted that organizations focused on family ministries were more likely to have women in leadership than were organizations that focused on missions or discipleship ministries.[25] Finally, at the time of the study, among Christian colleges and universities women made up only 5 percent of presidents and 20 percent of provosts, compared to national averages of 26 percent and 40 percent, respectively.[26] When Christian organizations actively or passively limit women's presence to lower-level and support roles, they communicate that women are less important and have less to contribute to the organizational mission than men do.

Underpaid and Expected to Volunteer

A related problem is women's unequal pay or lack of pay for similar work as their male counterparts. Indeed, an abundance of research has shown that women of all races and professions earn less than men, and the gap actually worsened in 2024.[27] Yet women's earnings are not optional or a luxury, as some think. More women than men live below the poverty line, both in the US and globally.[28] Still, some Christian organizations are not

24. Curry and Reynolds, *Missional Effectiveness*, 4.

25. Curry and Reynolds, *Missional Effectiveness*, 5.

26. Curry and Reynolds, *Missional Effectiveness*, 5.

27. Erin George and Gretchen Livingston, "What You Need to Know About the Gender Wage Gap," originally posted to *U.S. Department of Labor*, March 12, 2024, now viewable at https://www.workplacefairness.org/what-you-need-to-know-about-the-gender-wage-gap/; Marianne Cooper and Priya Fielding-Singh, "Younger Women's Experiences Show Gender Equity at Work Isn't Inevitable," *Harvard Business Review*, November 1, 2024, https://hbr.org/2024/11/younger-womens-experiences-show-gender-equity-at-work-isnt-inevitable; Miranda Peterson, "The Unfinished Fight for Equal Pay: How Women Fared in 2024," Institute for Women's Policy Research, December 19, 2024, https://iwpr.org/the-unfinished-fight-for-equal-pay-how-women-fared-in-2024/.

28. *Poverty Rates for Adults Ages 19–64 by Sex*, Kaiser Family Foundation, 2023, https://www.kff.org/other/state-indicator/adult-poverty-rate-by-sex/;

notably better than their secular counterparts. A recent study conducted by Lifeway, for example, showed that of 842 women ministry leaders who responded to Lifeway's survey, a whopping 83 percent of them serve in unpaid roles. Only 9 percent are in a paid part-time role, and only 8 percent in a paid full-time role.[29] For churches with over 500 members, the number of paid leaders rises to 29 percent in full-time positions and 24 percent in part-time positions, meaning that almost half are still unpaid.[30] Additionally, only 14 percent of those women leaders have received seminary training.[31] Aaron Earls and Marissa Sullivan, who wrote the web release of the study, commented that women "lead sacrificially, with more than 4 in 5 (835) serving as volunteers or unpaid staff members."[32] It is sacrificial, but the lack of financial support is devaluing, as Jen Wilkin explains: "Churches value what they commit their wallets to. Lack of investment communicates that ministry to women is 'nice but not necessary.'"[33] Not paying women for their work certainly communicates that it is not highly valued. Beth Allison Barr has stronger words in response to the lack of pay. She notes that the report shows how women are vitally important to church health. Pointing out the heavy representation of Southern Baptist churches reflected in the report, she writes, "The same convention who voted in a landslide to disfellowship churches

Einar H. Dyvik, *Gender Poverty Gaps Worldwide in 2020 and 2021 (with a Forecast to 2030), by Gender*, Statista, accessed March 28, 2025, https://www.statista .com/statistics/1219896/gender-poverty-gaps-worldwide-by-gender/.

29. *State of Ministry to Women: Leaders Report*, Lifeway Research, accessed March 28, 2025, https://research.lifeway.com/state-of-ministry-to-women/, p. 5.

30. Jen Wilkin, "Honor Thy Church Mothers—with Wages," *Christianity Today*, October 2023, https://www.christianitytoday.com/2023/09/wilkin-women -ministry-leaders-church-staff-wages-lifeway/.

31. *State of Ministry to Women*, 55.

32. Aaron Earls and Marissa Postell Sullivan, "Churchgoers and Leaders Find Value in Ministry to Women," Lifeway Research, October 17, 2023, https://re search.lifeway.com/2023/10/17/churchgoers-and-leaders-find-value-in-ministry -to-women/.

33. Wilkin, "Honor Thy Church Mothers—with Wages," 4.

with women pastors not only heavily depends on female labor but does not financially compensate the female leaders they allow to serve."[34] In sum, women "often serve without recognition, without compensation, and without resources."[35] Yet when Christian organizations fail to pay women or underpay them, they clearly communicate to women that their work is not significant enough to warrant full financial commitment. In other words, they are ambivalent about its value.

Benevolent Sexism

All of the issues described up to this point likely stem from sexist attitudes that are baked into Christian organizations. When the topic of sexism comes up, people may think of overtly hostile attitudes or name-calling addressed toward women.[36] Christian organizations may assume that if such actions and speech are not part of their organization, then sexism is not present. But sexism can take other, more innocuous-seeming forms.

Benevolent sexism is a kind of patronizing attitude toward women, seeing them as childlike or needing to be protected. It "consists of seemingly chivalrous comments and behavior based on stereotypical assumptions about women."[37] Pet names, not using titles, credibility deficit, and lack of support likely all stem from benevolent sexist attitudes. Additionally, benevolent sexism may be happening when men think they are protecting women at work—for example, not offering a work

34. Beth Allison Barr, "Why Do We Devalue Women's Work in Christian Institutions?," Substack, October 19, 2023, https://bethallisonbarr.substack.com /p/why-do-we-devalue-womens-work-in.

35. Wilkin, "Honor Thy Church Mothers—with Wages," 4.

36. In the wake of the 2024 presidential election, hostile sexism toward women has experienced a resurgence. See Isabelle Francis-Wright and Moustafa Ayad, "'Your Body, My Choice': Hate and Harassment Towards Women Spreads Online," Institute for Strategic Dialogue, November 8, 2024, https://www.isdglobal .org/digital_dispatches/your-body-my-choice-hate-and-harassment-towards -women-spreads-online/.

37. Diehl and Dzubinski, *Glass Walls*, 107.

trip to a woman because men assume she would prefer to stay home with her family. But assuming a woman will not want to travel for work robs her of agency to make her own decision. Studies show that, whether through patronizing behavior, compliments, or offering women unsolicited help, benevolent sexist acts reduce women's cognitive performance.[38] The effect at work, then, is that women in benevolent sexist environments need to spend energy and time first rejecting the patronizing messages before they can focus on doing their work. Their lost time and energy mean lost productivity for the organization.

Sanctified Sexism

A particularly pernicious form of sexism in Christian institutions is what Elizabeth Hall, Brad Christerson, and Shelly Cunningham call "sanctified sexism."[39] By that they mean gender schemas based on religion that are used to justify sexist treatment of women.[40] Or in simpler language, people use religion to justify biased treatment of females. Consider the man who tells his female colleague, "I am praying your husband can make more money so you can stay home with your children." What seems to start like a kind comment (I am praying for you) quickly becomes a message to the woman that her choice to work is wrong and that she belongs at home. In their study of a Christian university, the researchers found that religiously motivated statements that felt derogatory to the recipient diminished her sense of being influential and her sense of being informed. Worse, the statements felt unchangeable and

---

38. Rotem Kahalon, Nurit Shnabel, and Julia C. Becker, "'Don't Bother Your Pretty Little Head': Appearance Compliments Lead to Improved Mood but Impaired Cognitive Performance," *Psychology of Women Quarterly* 42, no. 2 (2018): 136–37, 41, 45–46.

39. M. Elizabeth Lewis Hall, Brad Christerson, and Shelly Cunningham, "Sanctified Sexism: Religious Beliefs and the Gender Harassment of Academic Women," *Psychology of Women Quarterly* 34, no. 2 (2010): 181.

40. Hall, Christerson, and Cunningham, "Sanctified Sexism," 182.

unchallengeable. Sanctified sexism, then, has the same negative cognitive impact as benevolent sexism, and it additionally robs women of the ability to push back against the demeaning messages. Since the message has been attributed to God, resisting the message feels the same as resisting God.

Scripture's Perspective

The church does not have a very good track record in terms of believing in women's value and worth. Possibly, twenty-first century women in the Western church have the best situation since the New Testament church and the early centuries. Jesus called women, spoke with women, taught women, accepted women as disciples, and generally treated women, in Dorothy Sayers's famous words, "as human."[41] But it was not long before church fathers and church councils reverted to seeing women the way their cultures saw women, ways that viewed them as less valuable than men.[42] While taking different forms in different time periods, that belief has persisted to the present day. In the last fifty to sixty years, progress has been made, but the challenges discussed in this chapter show that even the best churches and organizations still have room to improve. Let's take a look at some biblical texts to see that God is not ambivalent toward women.

Created in God's Image

Genesis 1:26–27 describes how God created human beings.

Then God said, "Let us make humans in our image, according to our likeness, and let them have dominion over the fish of the

41. Dorothy L. Sayers, *Are Women Human? Penetrating, Sensible, and Witty Essays on the Role of Women in Society* (Eerdmans, 1971).
42. Dzubinski and Stasson, *Women in the Mission of the Church*, 21–23; Mathews, *Gender Roles and the People of God*, 161–70.

sea and over the birds of the air and over the cattle and over
all the wild animals of the earth and over every creeping thing
that creeps upon the earth."
So God created humans in his image,
    in the image of God he created them;
    male and female he created them.

In the creation narrative, there is no distinction in value and
worth between the male and the female. Both are created in
God's image, and both are given the same work (as was discussed in chap. 3). Although some early church fathers saw
women as not bearing the whole image of God or as reflecting
a defective or partial image, the Bible does not support such a
belief.[43] And indeed the church has come to reject such thinking
as theologically incorrect.

One in Christ's Body

Paul also explains the unity of followers of Jesus, describing Christians as "one body." Both Romans and 1 Corinthians
express similar thoughts. In Romans, Paul writes, "For as in one
body we have many members and not all the members have the
same function, so we, who are many, are one body in Christ,
and individually we are members one of another" (12:4–5). The
language in 1 Corinthians is similar: "For just as the body is
one and has many members, and all the members of the body,
though many, are one body, so it is with Christ. For in the one
Spirit we were all baptized into one body—Jews or Greeks,
slaves or free—and we were all made to drink of one Spirit"
(12:12–13). In this passage Paul notes the unity of two of the
important social divisions of his day: slaves versus free people
and Jews versus Greeks. In Galatians 3:28 he adds gender to
the mix, saying, "There is no Jew-Greek division, there is no

43. Dzubinski and Stasson, *Women in the Mission of the Church*, 2–3, 23;
Mathews, *Gender Roles and the People of God*, 161, 64–66, 68–70, 74–77.

slave-free division, there is no male-female division, for you are all one in Christ Jesus."[44] Philip Payne describes the significance of these expressions of unity: "Paul's point is that gender, just as race and social rank, is irrelevant to status in Christ. Just as gentiles should have the same opportunities for service in the church as Jews, and slaves should have the same opportunities for service in the church as free persons, women should also have the same opportunities for service in the church as men."[45] According to Paul, all followers of Jesus are one body and are one in Jesus, and social and class distinctions no longer matter. God shows no ambivalence toward women.

Additionally, all believers are called a holy priesthood, as Peter wrote: "But you are a chosen people, a royal priesthood, a holy nation, God's own people, in order that you may proclaim the excellence of him who called you out of darkness into his marvelous light" (1 Pet. 2:9). God's people, united as one in the body of Christ across all social divisions, are together a chosen, royal, holy people who exist to proclaim God's greatness. Some are not more important than others; women are not less valuable than men in God's kingdom.

God Speaks to Women

God clearly thinks, and biblical stories show, that women are credible and should be taken seriously. Consider the story told in Judges 13 of a nameless woman who is married to a man named Manoah. Manoah belonged to the tribe of Daniel and was living in Zorah at the time the story begins. The woman has no children, and one day an angel appears to her and tells her she is going to have a son. The angel gives specific instructions about her own self-care during pregnancy and about how to raise the child. While pregnant, she is not to drink any alcoholic

---

44. Translation by Philip Payne, *The Bible vs. Biblical Womanhood: How God's Word Consistently Affirms Gender Equality* (Zondervan, 2023), 103.
45. Payne, *The Bible vs. Biblical Womanhood*, 104–5.

beverages or eat anything unclean. The child will be a boy, and he is to be raised as a Nazirite, including never having a haircut (Judg. 13:1–5). The angel promises that her son will deliver Israel from the Philistines (v. 5). When she tells her husband about the visit, it seems he may not quite believe her, because he turns around and asks God to send the angel back "to us" to "teach us" what to do (v. 8). He wants to hear the news for himself. What happens next is both funny and ironic: "God listened to Manoah, and the angel of God came again to the woman as she sat in the field; but her husband Manoah was not with her" (v. 9). God seems to think that the woman is perfectly capable of hearing and following the angel's instructions. Still, she goes to get her husband, who then quizzes the angel to see if what his wife had told him was correct. It was, of course. The angel patiently repeats all the instructions for this man who doubts his own wife. After the angel leaves, the man has a complete meltdown, saying, "We are doomed to die! . . . We have seen God" (v. 22 NIV). His practical wife points out that God would hardly have accepted their offering and given them such clear instructions about her pregnancy only to kill them. Her faith is completely correct: They live, and she does have a son, Samson, who judges Israel for twenty years (16:31).[46] This woman who has no name and is known only by her relationships to her husband and son is nevertheless completely worthy of receiving God's message and sharing it correctly with those who need to hear it. Two times God was willing to entrust this important message to this nameless woman, clearly finding her capable of receiving, understanding, and acting on the instructions.

Manoah's wife is not the only woman in Scripture who heard directly from God about what she should do, either. Hagar heard from God when she was sitting by the well, having run

46. The whole story of Samson is told in Judg. 13–16.

away from Sarah who was abusing her. The angel told her to return to Sarah and promised her that through her son, Ishmael, her descendants would be so many they could not be counted (Gen. 16:10). The angel also comforted her, assuring her that God had seen her abuse (16:11). A few chapters later, when Sarah overheard the angel telling Abraham that he would have a son by her, she laughed. The angel asked why she laughed, and when she denied it, responded to her, "Yes, you did laugh" (18:15).[47] God also confronted Eve directly about eating the fruit, not just Adam (3:13). And God spoke to prophets Huldah and Deborah, giving them the prophecies their people needed to hear.[48]

In the New Testament, Mary heard directly from the angel Gabriel and had a lengthy conversation with him about God's plan for her (Luke 1:28–38). At the tomb when Jesus has been raised, the angels speak directly to "Mary Magdalene, Joanna, Mary the mother of James, and the other women" (Luke 24:10) with the famous words, "Why do you look for the living among the dead? He is not here but has risen" (v. 5). God shows no ambivalence when communicating with women.

Jesus Speaks Through Women

Jesus himself also entrusted his message to women on several occasions. John 4 records the encounter with the Samaritan woman at the well. While preaching throughout the centuries has tended to characterize this woman as fallen and sinful, little different from a prostitute, such thinking is not the only interpretation and has been contested by various theologians

---

47. Interestingly, in Gen. 17, when God tells Abraham that Sarah will bear a son, Abraham also laughed (v. 17). In much popular teaching, Sarah's laugh is treated as a sign of disbelief, but Abraham's laugh is completely ignored.

48. Huldah reports God's word using the classic formula "thus says the LORD" in 2 Kings 22:15–16 and 2 Chron. 34:23–24. Deborah reports God's word to Barak, saying, "The LORD, the God of Israel, commands you" in Judg. 4:6.

over the centuries.[49] First, the idea that she came to the well at the middle of the day to avoid other women is unsupported. It is far more likely that she is coming in the evening at the normal time to draw water. While the Synoptic Gospels appear to use Jewish time (two twelve-hour periods running from 6 a.m. to 6 p.m. and 6 p.m. to 6 a.m.), John appears to use Roman time (like our current system of starting to count at midnight and starting again at noon). So the woman was coming to the well at evening, not noon.[50] Furthermore, the likelihood of the disciples stopping for lunch instead of in the evening is also low. They would have packed a lunch for their walk and only stopped when it was getting dark and they had eaten their provisions.[51] Second, women in the first century did not have much ability to divorce a husband; divorce was typically the prerogative of men.[52] One possible explanation for her series of husbands is infertility. If she were unable to conceive, that would be grounds for a husband to divorce her. Another likely explanation is that several husbands had died; after all it was

49. See Lynn H. Cohick, "The 'Woman at the Well': Was the Samaritan Woman Really an Adulteress?," in *Vindicating the Vixens: Revisiting the Sexualized, Vilified, and Marginalized Women of the Bible*, ed. Sandra Glahn (Kregel Academic, 2017), 249–54. A fuller treatment is offered by Caryn A. Reeder, *The Samaritan Woman's Story: Reconsidering John 4 After #Churchtoo* (IVP, 2022).

50. According to Ronald C. Christie, "If you accept the Roman view, there is nothing difficult to explain [about when the woman goes to draw water]. It is the end of a working day. Jesus is, not unnaturally, tired from his long journey; the disciples, not unnaturally, have gone to find food; and the woman, not unnaturally, is drawing water in connection with the evening meal." Ronald C. Christie, "John's Gospel: Counting Time," *The Monthly Record* (1993), https://www.christianstudylibrary.org/article/johns-gospel-counting-time.

51. See Matt. 14:13–21. First, food was needed in the evening. Second, the twelve disciples picked up twelve baskets of leftovers, one for each of them. "So much was left over that each of the twelve disciples gathered food in his wicker foodbasket (sources may suggest that Jewish workers often carried their meals in these)." Craig S. Keener, *The Gospel of Matthew: A Socio-Rhetorical Commentary* (Eerdmans, 2009), 405.

52. Cohick, "'Woman at the Well'?," 250; Dorothy A. Lee, *The Ministry of Women in the New Testament: Reclaiming the Biblical Vision for Church Leadership* (Baker Academic, 2021), 83.

common for women to be married to older men.[53] Additionally, the fact that she was living with someone to whom she was not married shows that husband number five did not die and might have been cruel. Instead of providing a divorce, he seems to have just thrown her out, leaving her unable to marry again. In all likelihood her father and brothers—if she had any—are dead, since they would have been the ones to take her in and care for her. Rather than see her as a self-willed serial adulteress, this woman should be seen through eyes of compassion as a woman whose social system had totally failed her. By moving in with a man she cannot marry, she accepts the only male protection she can find.[54]

In this context, her spiritual knowledge and insight are striking. She understands the theological differences between her Samaritan people and the wider Jewish population. She quickly discerns that Jesus is a prophet and immediately asks him the most pressing theological question of her day: Where is the right place to worship?[55] And Jesus takes her question completely seriously. He responds that worship is not about a location but about worshiping "the Father in spirit and truth" (John 4:23). She adds that she knows the Messiah is coming, and Jesus responds with the classic two-word name for God, "I am" (v. 26).[56] Her response is instant belief. She is so certain of this information that she leaves her water pot, the water pot that was utterly necessary for her physical survival, and runs back to town to call everyone to come meet Jesus (vv. 19–29). Early church writers like Chrysostom recognized her

53. Cohick, "'Woman at the Well'?," 251–52.
54. Lee, *Ministry of Women*, 83.
55. Lee, *Ministry of Women*, 83.
56. The name "I AM" comes from Exod. 3:14, where God reveals this name to Moses. Jesus uses the phrase ἐγώ εἰμί as a freestanding clause here and again of himself in John 8:58 and 18:6. Most English translations of these verses add an additional "he" (I am he) making it difficult for readers to see the significance of the phrase.

evangelism. He comments, "Observe her zeal and wisdom. . . . She of her own accord, without the command of any, leaves her water pot, and winged by joy performs the office of Evangelists."[57] Rather than the whiny, evasive, sinful adulteress so often presented, she is better seen as a woman who had suffered deep pain, asked key theological questions, believed in God, and made sure everyone she knew could also come to a knowledge of the truth.

Another instance of Jesus entrusting women with his message happens at the resurrection. As all four Gospels report, it is the women who first go to the tomb, first see the risen Jesus, and first proclaim his resurrection to the other disciples (Matt. 28:9–10; Mark 16:9–10; Luke 24:10; John 20:14–18). Among the women named in every account is Mary Magdalene, who had been freed from seven demons (Luke 8:2). Despite the reputational ruin she suffered later, Mary Magdalene was not a prostitute; she was the first to see the risen Lord.[58] She is known as the "apostle to the apostles" for her faithful witness.[59]

These examples show that God does not think women lack credibility. To the contrary, God is perfectly willing to speak to and through women to share his plans. And based on these stories, God expected the men around these women to accept their word and believe their testimony.

Taken together, the scriptural evidence is clear. God shows no ambivalence toward women. God does not regard women

57. John Chrysostom, "Homily 34," in *Homilies on the Gospel of John*, https://www.newadvent.org/fathers/240134.htm.

58. Lee, *Ministry of Women*, 84.

59. Lee, *Ministry of Women*, 88. Thomas Aquinas says of Mary Magdalene: "Thirdly, she had the office of an apostle; indeed, she was *an apostle to the apostles* insofar as it was her task to announce our Lord's resurrection to the disciples." Thomas Aquinas, Lecture 3 on John 20, in *Commentary on the Gospel of St. John*, trans. James A. Weisheipl (Magi Books, 1998), para. 2519 (emphasis added), https://isidore.co/aquinas/english/SSJohn.htm.

as less credible, less trustworthy, or less valuable than men. To the contrary, God entrusts women with important messages, sends them as apostles, and engages in self-revelation to women. Christian organizations should be the first to recognize the problematic nature of perpetuating ambivalent attitudes toward women and to use good theology to create spaces where women as well as men can thrive.

Strategies to Eliminate Ambivalence

As in the previous chapter, there are straightforward strategies to combat ambivalence toward women, and there are also deeper cultural changes needed. First, I will name some straightforward strategies, and then I will discuss deeper level cultural change.

Do a Language Audit

For the hurtful language practices presented earlier in this chapter, organizations can do an audit to see to what degree they engage in such practices, and then work to set clear norms and standards for different language. Start by listening for pet names. Are women being addressed with language like "honey" or "dear" or "sweetheart"? Check for the use of pet names for employees and also for members and constituents of an organization. All such uses are problematic. Call attention to them and then require professional language in the workplace instead.

Similarly, watch out for untitling and uncredentialing, whether of organizational employees or of constituents. Check your church bulletin and organizational communications. Are women's titles and credentials being used the same way men's are? Similarly, take a look at your mailing list. Are women's credentials used similarly to men's? Do alumni newsletters go to "Rev. and Mrs. Jones" even when she has an earned credential?

Well-addressed mail will include her titles as well as his: "Dr. Robert Attipoe and Dr. Aneesha Attipoe," not "Dr. and Mrs. Attipoe." Women have significant financial power and often influence or decide about charitable giving. Organizations that depend on donations may want to be doubly vigilant that they are not needlessly insulting their women donors by neglecting titles and credentials.

The organizational language audit can also look for ways women are subject to credibility deficit. Are women's statements believed from the start, or has a culture of disbelief grown up? Do women have to do extra work not expected of men to support their points and ideas? Evidence and support are good, but the problem is when they are demanded of women in ways not expected of men. Spend some time observing meetings and reports to see if the standards are the same. If not, set clear standards for the whole organization about the kind and amount of support required for reports, decisions, and the like.

Examine Support Structures

Consider how your organizational support structures work. Are women provided with sufficient resources to do their jobs? Do they have the necessary budget, personnel, and administrative support for the work they have been asked to do? Or are they perhaps expected to do their own administrative work while male colleagues are provided with support staff? Also consider authority: When a leader asks a woman to do something, does that leader then have her back in getting the job done and supporting her if she is challenged? Do leaders take the word of male subordinates (like the second opening story in this chapter) and make decisions without the woman's knowledge? Finally, do people disagree with or correct women? Are such comments made publicly with women but not with men? All of these practices communicate ambivalence to women, and all should be eliminated from organizational practices. Ensure women receive all the resources they need and on par with their male colleagues. Ensure they can rely on the leaders above them to support them when they do their jobs, and do not correct or shame them publicly if they make a mistake.

Next, audit pay scales for equity. If women are being paid less than men for similar work, fix it. Do not allow gendered excuses like "he has a family to support" to influence rates of pay. Women also work to support their families and themselves. Make sure opportunities for overtime and bonus work, travel, continuing education, and similar job perquisites are equally offered to women and men.

Work on Theology

Because many of these practices do stem from benevolent and sanctified sexist beliefs, some deeper work at the theological level may also be required. For example, it could help to hold a Bible study on what it means to be God's image bearers or what it means to be coheirs with Christ. Sermons and discussions on women like the nameless wife of Manoah, Hagar, Sarah, the Samaritan woman, and the women who followed Jesus should be addressed to the entire congregation or organization and not just reserved for women's groups. Second Timothy 3:16–17 states, "All scripture is inspired by God and is useful for teaching, for reproof, for correction, and for training in righteousness, so that the person of God may be proficient, equipped for every good work." Stories of women are included in the Bible for the benefit of all members of the church, male and female alike.

Organizational leaders must set the tone and standards in these areas, just like the problems of work culture discussed in the previous chapter. This kind of work is going to take longer and needs to be done prayerfully. Yet the results, in terms of healthy organizational climates where women as well as men can flourish, will be well worth the effort.

Chapter Summary

This chapter has examined a number of ways women find themselves treated with ambivalence at work. From language that patronizes and communicates that women belong in the home to not being supported or paid fairly, organizations can easily communicate to women that they simply do not matter as much as men. Yet Scripture in no way supports the cultural view that women are of less value than men. Rather, it is full of stories showing that God values women and is in no way ambivalent toward them. Organizations that want to create flourishing environments and benefit from all the wisdom and skill that women bring to the workplace will need to work diligently to root out cultural beliefs and practices that devalue women. They also need to work on rooting out underlying attitudes of benevolent and sanctified sexism. The work may be challenging, but the results will be well worth the effort.

5

"There Are No Good Women Leaders"

The Power of Social Role Stereotypes

How can I use my gift of leadership in a Christian organization?
—missionary woman[1]

He would use anger to try and get me to capitulate, or break down, or withdraw, or whatever.
—mission leader speaking about one of her direct reports[2]

M any years ago when I was serving with a mission organization, I asked one of the male leaders why there were no women on the leadership team. I was stunned when

1. Leanne M. Dzubinski, "Portrayal vs. Practice: Contemporary Women's Contributions to Christian Mission," *Missiology: An International Review* 44, no. 1 (2016): 87.
2. This quotation was collected as part of my own research that has not yet been published and is quoted by permission of the interviewee.

97

he responded that there simply were no good female leaders. Yet I could see the good potential women leaders all around me, if they had been given an opportunity. Over the years I have learned that his perspective is not unusual. The comment is common enough that most women in Christian organizations that I talk with have heard some version of it.

I have also heard male leaders say that women do not want to lead. "I asked one," they would say, "and she said no." One or two experiences of a woman saying no can cause male leaders to conclude that women do not want to lead. Yet when I studied women in mission organizations, I found a significant level of frustration at the lack of opportunities they had for leadership.[3]

On the other hand, women do sometimes resist offers of leadership. One mission leader told me, "I was completely un-prepared for [the board's request that I become CEO]. I started telling them all the reasons why they were wrong, and how I was certainly not the right person for that role, and all the reasons why I wasn't interested in taking it."[4] Another mission leader said, "I asked for an interim assignment because I wasn't sure I could do it."[5] In both cases, these women initially advocated against themselves for the role they were being asked to fill. In both cases, their leaders worked with them to understand their initial reluctance and then to create pathways enabling them to take the job and flourish in it.

What is going on that makes it difficult for men to see tal-ented women leaders around them? And what is going on that makes it difficult for some women to see themselves as leaders? This chapter answers those questions by looking at cultural and

3. Dzubinski, "Portrayal vs. Practice," 87.

4. Amy B. Diehl and Leanne M. Dzubinski, "Making the Invisible Visible: A Cross-Sector Analysis of Gender-Based Leadership Barriers," *Human Resource Development Quarterly* 27, no. 2 (2016): 192.

5. Leanne M. Dzubinski, *Playing by the Rules: How Women Lead in Evangeli-cal Mission Organizations*, American Society of Missiology Monograph Series 52 (Pickwick, 2021), 173.

Christian ideas of leadership, masculinity, femininity, roles, and stereotypes. It also offers suggestions for how organizations and leaders can change their perspectives of men, women, and leadership. Finally, I recommend ways male leaders can help a woman arrive at "yes" when offered a leadership role.

Think Leader, Think Male

In 1973, Virginia Schein studied three hundred male managers' perceptions of what makes a good middle manager. She found that "successful middle managers are perceived to possess those characteristics, attitudes and temperaments more commonly ascribed to men in general than to women in general."[6] The connection was so strong it was dubbed the "think manager, think male" effect. Subsequent studies in the 1990s showed that the effect continued, and that it was a global phenomenon.[7] The studies showed that although women's attitudes shifted over time to see women as "more likely to hold some traits necessary for success," men's opinions had not changed.[8] The same persistence in men's attitudes was found globally.[9]

Schein's work leads to a question: What is it about men and women that causes people to assume that men make good leaders, but women do not? The answer has turned out to be society's gender role stereotypes about what makes a good man and a good woman. Fundamentally, society associates certain qualities

6. Virginia Ellen Schein, "The Relationship Between Sex Role Stereotypes and Requisite Management Characteristics," *Journal of Applied Psychology* 57, no. 2 (1973): 99.

7. O. C. Brenner, Joseph Tomkiewicz, and Virginia Ellen Schein, "The Relationship Between Sex Role Stereotypes and Requisite Management Characteristics Revisited," *Academy of Management Journal* 32, no. 3 (1989): 668; Virginia Ellen Schein et al., "Think Manager—Think Male: A Global Phenomenon?," *Journal of Organizational Behavior* 17 (1996): 33.

8. Brenner, Tomkiewicz, and Schein, "Relationship Between Sex Role Stereotypes and Requisite Management Characteristics Revisited," 688.

9. Schein et al., "Think Manager—Think Male," 39.

with men and other, seemingly opposite, qualities with women. Men's qualities are agentic: being directive, decisive, in control, confident, and assertive. These are highly task-oriented qualities. Women's qualities, on the other hand, are communal: nurturing, relational, supportive, kind, submissive. They are highly relationship-oriented qualities.[10] These qualities are viewed as both descriptive and prescriptive. Descriptively, they depict how society believes men and women behave. Prescriptively, they describe how men and women should behave, and they can be used to punish those who deviate from the expectations.[11] So calling boys or men "sissies" or "weak" is a way of encouraging them to stick with the assumed male qualities. And calling women "aggressive" or "outspoken" is a way of pushing them back into the desired female qualities of submission and quietness.

The next layer of the puzzle is social expectations of leader behavior. Most leadership theory agrees that good leaders need to achieve tasks or get things done. There is also recognition that leaders need to take care of the people in the organization.[12] Yet that need is typically seen as secondary to getting things done. Since men are assumed to be good at taking charge and women at taking care, men are therefore seen as better leaders.[13] Men are the ones, presumably, who will be best at getting things

10. Alice H. Eagly and Steven J. Karau, "Role Congruity Theory of Prejudice Toward Female Leaders," *Psychological Review* 109, no. 3 (2002): 574.

11. Eagly and Karau, "Role Congruity Theory of Prejudice," 574.

12. The two main responsibilities of leaders, being task oriented and people oriented, were first identified in the 1950s in two separate sets of studies. Interestingly, the studies were conducted only with men. See Ralph M. Stogdill and Alvin E. Coons, eds., *Leader Behavior: Its Description and Measurement*, Ohio Studies in Personnel 88 (The Ohio State University, 1957); Daniel Katz et al., *Productivity, Supervision and Morale Among Raliroad Workers* (University of Michigan, 1951).

13. The phrase "women take care, men take charge" is an updated version of the "think manager, think male" sentiment. Jeanine L. Prime, Nancy M. Carter, and Theresa M. Welbourne, "Women 'Take Care,' Men 'Take Charge': Managers' Stereotypic Perceptions of Women and Men Leaders," *Psychologist-Manager Journal* 12, no. 1 (2009): 25–49.

done. Women, presumably, will focus primarily on taking care of people and only secondarily on getting things done. Thus, stereotypes for men and for leaders align closely, while stereotypes for women and leaders do not match. Hence men are assumed to be better leaders. Table 1 compares the social role stereotypes for men, leaders, and women.

Table 1
Social Role Stereotypes and Leader Stereotypes

Men	Leaders	Women
Directive	Set vision and direction	Nurturing
Decisive	Make decisions	Relational
In control	Be in charge	Supportive
Confident	Confident	Kind
Assertive	Assertive	Submissive
Task oriented	Task oriented	Relationship oriented
AGENTIC	AGENTIC	COMMUNAL

Of course these are stereotypes that do not reflect the reality of any given person. Men may be very good at taking care of others, and women may be very good at getting things done. The care and raising of children is just one example of an area where women may show excellent managerial skills. In Ann Crittenden's famous words, "If you've raised kids, you can manage anything."[14]

Still, it is easy to see how these stereotypes operate at work and in leadership roles. If men "take charge" and women "take care" and if the primary responsibility of leaders is to "take charge," then clearly men would seem to be the better leaders. Or, as Olle Folke and colleagues put it, "Leadership is generally considered a male activity, making a man the prototypical

14. Ann Crittenden, *If You've Raised Kids, You Can Manage Anything: Leadership Begins at Home* (Gotham Books, 2004).

manager and a woman manager a deviation from the norm."[15] In fact, research and data from forty-plus years show that these beliefs continue to operate.[16] And these stereotypes are the most common explanation for why, even well into the twenty-first century, there are so few women at the top of organizational hierarchies. Manuela Tremmel and Ingrid Wahl explain, "Stereotypical masculine characteristics are still seen as key prerequisites for successful leadership."[17] They add that stereotypical female qualities are seen as nice to have but not necessary.[18]

The final layer of the puzzle is how stereotypes work, both descriptively and prescriptively, as already mentioned. When these stereotypes operate in a prescriptive manner—being viewed as requirements for men and women—they create what is known as a double-bind for women in positions of leadership.[19] Fundamentally, agentic and communal qualities are perceived as opposites: "They contradict each other (e.g., demanding and caring, authoritative and participative)."[20] In order to be viewed as good leaders, women need to demonstrate the agentic qualities that are seen as essential to the leader role. However, by exhibiting those agentic qualities, they are perceived as lacking in the communal qualities required of women and are disliked.[21] Race and ethnicity further compli-

15. Olle Folke et al., "Sexual Harassment of Women Leaders," *Daedalus, the Journal of the American Academy of Arts & Sciences* 149, no. 1 (2020): 189.

16. Chidinma Favour Chikwe, Nkechi Emmanuella Eneh, and Chidiogo Uzoamaka Akpuokwe, "Navigating the Double Bind: Strategies for Women Leaders in Overcoming Stereotypes and Leadership Biases," *GSC Advanced Research and Reviews* 18, no. 3 (2024): 160; Sanne Feenstra et al., "Managerial Stereotypes Over Time: The Rise of Feminine Leadership," *Gender in Management: An International Journal* 38, no. 6 (2023): 771; Manuela Tremmel and Ingrid Wahl, "Gender Stereotypes in Leadership: Analysing the Content and Evaluation of Stereotypes About Typical, Male, and Female Leaders," *Frontiers in Psychology* 14 (2023): 1.

17. Tremmel and Wahl, "Gender Stereotypes in Leadership," 3.

18. Tremmel and Wahl, "Gender Stereotypes in Leadership," 3.

19. Tremmel and Wahl, "Gender Stereotypes in Leadership," 2.

20. Tremmel and Wahl, "Gender Stereotypes in Leadership," 2.

21. Folke et al., "Sexual Harassment of Women Leaders," 189.

cate matters, as "black women are often penalized for being too masculine, . . . [and] Asian women are often characterized as too submissive."[22] In short, women can be viewed as "good women" or "good leaders" but not both.

When the stereotypes are seen as both required and mutually exclusive, people will struggle to see women as good leaders. Men may have trouble recognizing the leadership potential of women in their organization. Some men, like the subordinate who used anger to resist his woman leader, may flat-out reject women's leadership. And some women may struggle to recognize their own capacity to lead, as did the woman in the opening quotation.

Evangelical Gender Role Stereotypes

In the previous chapter I said that women in the twenty-first century may have it best in church since the earliest days of the Christian community, before Christianity became an official religion under Constantine. Unfortunately, in the area of gender stereotypes, Christianity has not done much to counter these social messages. In fact, rather like their Victorian predecessors of the 1800s, who taught that separate spheres was God's design for humanity, evangelical preachers and teachers of the 1970s and 1980s took cultural values and baptized them into the Christian faith, declaring them to be God's ideal for human relationships.[23]

---

22. Rachel D. Godsil et al. *The Science of Equality*, vol. 2, *The Effects of Gender Roles, Implicit Bias, and Stereotype Threat on the Lives of Women and Girls* (Perception Institute, 2016), 29.

23. See chap. 3 for a discussion of separate spheres. Clergy took the social message and presented it as biblical. For more on how "biblical womanhood" was created, see Beth Allison Barr, *The Making of Biblical Womanhood: How the Subjugation of Women Became Gospel Truth* (Brazos, 2021). See also Kristin Kobes Du Mez, *Jesus and John Wayne: How White Evangelicals Corrupted a Faith and Fractured a Nation* (Liveright, 2020).

In the early 1980s, some male evangelical leaders were concerned with what they saw as women's increasing presence and power in society. Framing their concerns around family values, they created a gender schema they called "biblical manhood and biblical womanhood." Promoted by The Council for Biblical Manhood and Womanhood (CBMW), the schema argued that men and women have equal worth before God but are assigned to different roles in home, church, and society.[24] They wanted to avoid the mistakes of previous generations that had simply said women were inferior (see chap. 2) while still maintaining some degree of difference between them— difference, it turns out, that primarily focuses on power and authority. In their system, women are always barred in some way from the highest or most authoritative position in any organization, be it family, church, or society. Over time the view has morphed, and in some places societal restrictions have lessened, but home and church are two arenas where women are fundamentally restricted, because they are women, from a top leadership role. This theological view is known as complementarianism.[25]

In their writings, this group created descriptions of qualities and characteristics they considered suitable for women and for men. In retreat after retreat, I have asked women to list the qualities of a good Christian woman and a good Christian man. The lists are remarkably similar each time, and they are also remarkably similar to the social role stereotypes just described. Table 2 compares the social gender role stereotypes and the evangelical gender role stereotypes side by side. While the specific words may vary slightly, the general view of men as agentic and women as communal holds firm.

24. See their website: https://cbmw.org.
25. Wayne Grudem, "A Letter from Wayne Grudem," The Council on Biblical Manhood and Womanhood, September 28, 2020, https://cbmw.org/2020/09/28/a-letter-from-wayne-grudem.

The problem, of course, is that knowing about social role stereotypes makes it impossible not to see that evangelical gender roles match almost precisely to societal expectations. Rather than being a set of qualities for men and women that were derived from biblical teaching, they can be seen for what they are: social thinking about men and women that has been baptized into Christianity.[26]

Table 2
Social and Evangelical Gender Role Stereotypes

Social Gender Role Stereotypes		Evangelical Gender Roles	
Men	**Women**	**Man's Role**	**Woman's Role**
Assertive	Affectionate	Lead	Submit
Controlling	Nurturing	Spiritual authority	Caretaker
Confident	Kind	Make decisions	Support decisions
Task oriented	Relational	Get things done	Relational
Independent	Dependent	Independent	Dependent
Initiators	Followers/supporters	Initiator	Responder
AGENTIC	COMMUNAL	AGENTIC	COMMUNAL

Source: Leanne M. Dzubinski, "Taking on Power: Women Leaders in Evangelical Mission Organizations," *Missiology: An International Review* 44, no. 3 (2016): 283.

Of what value are these characteristics, then, if they do not truly define Christian men and Christian women? None of them are bad in themselves, yet when they are segregated into strict expectations based on gender and presented as biblical, they can indeed become harmful, especially when unthinkingly enacted in the workplace.

People are not stereotypes. As previously stated, men exhibit communal characteristics, and women exhibit agentic

26. The concepts of men as agentic and women as communal have been evident for centuries (see the discussion in the section "Separate Spheres" in chap. 3). These beliefs are based on gender essentialism (see the section titled "Gender Essentialist Thinking" in chap. 3).

characteristics. In fact, both types are needed for a well-rounded human being. But too often, people are not even aware that they hold these underlying beliefs. Or they have been told that the beliefs are Christian, and therefore questioning them seems sinful.

Consequences of Stereotypes

Allowing stereotypes to guide societal and organizational thinking has consequences. Thoughts matter; words matter. Operating out of unquestioned and unexamined beliefs means that organizational structures and practices and systems function in ways that have predictable outcomes for their members. In this section I will consider how operating based on stereotypes impacts women, including heightened gender prejudice, imbalances of power, and genderwashing.

Heightened Gender Prejudice

One consequence of embracing these social stereotypes is the perpetuation of prejudicial views of women, which further serve to privilege men. Research shows that "men devalue female leaders . . . and have more prejudices against female leaders than women [do]."[27] Many men also assume they are better leaders than women are.[28] Men who identify strongly with and affirm as correct stereotypical masculine characteristics described in this chapter also generally hold more sexist views of women and tend to support traditional gender

---

27. Tremmel and Wahl, "Gender Stereotypes in Leadership," 2.
28. Tremmel and Wahl, "Gender Stereotypes in Leadership," 2. Research has also found that men will apply for a job when they meet 60 percent of the required qualifications, whereas women will not apply unless they meet all the required qualifications. Tara Sophia Mohr, "Why Women Don't Apply for Jobs Unless They're 100% Qualified," *Harvard Business Review*, August 25, 2014, https://hbr.org/2014/08/why-women-dont-apply-for-jobs-unless-theyre-100-qualified.

roles.[29] Men in executive roles with stay-at-home wives may also strongly endorse traditional gender stereotypes, see women's employment as a personal choice, and fail to recognize that women may need to work for financial reasons.[30] Those attitudes have implications for the workplace. Such leaders may be unsympathetic to women's challenges at work and assume that women's problems are purely personal and not connected to workplace structures and systems.[31] They may be ambivalent about women's presence in the workplace to begin with.[32] These gender role stereotypes therefore have significant impact on women at work. And again, in a Christian organization where these stereotypes are presented as God's plan, the impact can be devastating for women.

Power and Its Potential for Abuse

Both social and Christian stereotypes privilege men over women by concentrating power and authority largely in male hands.[33] Philip Payne explains how limiting leadership to men creates power imbalances for Christians: "By 'gender hierarchy' I mean a power relationship between men and women in

29. Peter Glick, Mariah Wilkerson, and Marshall Cuffe, "Masculine Identity, Ambivalent Sexism, and Attitudes Toward Gender Subtypes: Favoring Masculine Men and Feminine Women," *Social Psychology* 46, no. 4 (2015): 210–11.

30. Sarah J. Tracy and Kendra Dyanne Rivera, "Endorsing Equity and Applauding Stay-At-Home Moms: How Male Voices on Work-Life Reveal Aversive Sexism and Flickers of Transformation," *Management Communication Quarterly* 24, no. 1 (2010): 27–28.

31. Tracy and Rivera, "Endorsing Equity," 27–28.

32. Tracy and Rivera, "Endorsing Equity," 27. Chapter 4 described how ambivalence toward women functions in the workplace and shows the consequences of not believing in women.

33. The CBMW website describes it this way: "the loving, humble leadership of redeemed husbands and the intelligent, willing support of that leadership by redeemed wives" ("The Danvers Statement," The Council on Biblical Manhood and Womanhood, https://cbmw.org/about/danvers-statement/). Although the words "loving" and "humble" qualify the relationship, the main focus is on leadership by men and the support role of women. The roles are neither mutual nor reversible.

which one gender is granted authority while the other is barred from serving in leadership roles. . . . In short, 'hierarchy' means uneven distribution of power."[34] He explains the connection further, saying,

> Now, some proponents of gender hierarchy *claim* that they believe men and women are equal: they are both made in the image of God, have equal worth in God's sight, and so on. But when it comes to the everyday practice of leadership and use of power, they do not treat women as equal to men. When certain leadership roles are *only and always* limited to men, that is by definition gender hierarchy—in fact it is a particular kind of gender hierarchy: patriarchy (rule by men).[35]

When social role stereotypes are translated into a gender schema that is taught as God's will for humanity, the power imbalance between men and women is also codified as God's will.

Many of the issues presented in this book stem from men's inherent social power. Men's use of a stained-glass partition to "protect" themselves from women, language that favors men and makes women invisible, work structures and cultures created by men with men's lifestyles and needs in mind, ambivalence toward women and their work contributions, and unconsciously or intentionally defining all women based on stereotypes are outcomes of male social power and privilege. Some men may want these outcomes, but many do not. Nevertheless, men's power is so thoroughly embedded in social and organizational functioning that it is rarely examined or questioned.

Before moving on, I want to pause to consider the dark side of unchecked power. When power and authority are unrestricted

---

34. Philip Barton Payne, *The Bible vs. Biblical Womanhood: How God's Word Consistently Affirms Gender Equality* (Zondervan, 2023), xxii.
35. Payne, *The Bible vs. Biblical Womanhood*, xxii (emphasis original).

and unchallengeable, the potential for abuse is real. It does not require much life experience to see the problems with unchecked power structures. The founders of the United States, some of whom were seeking to escape abusive power structures, built a system of government designed to prevent such a situation arising. Slavery is another example of the horrors of absolute power and authority of one group of people over another. Nazi Germany offers a similar salutary lesson, as do other totalitarian regimes. If one is tempted to dismiss those examples as not relevant for Christian organizations, consider some of the abuses brought to light over the past few years. There is the widespread abuse by Catholic clergy of children in their Pennsylvania dioceses.[36] Similarly, Catholic clergy were found to engage in widespread abuse of women religious, including forced domestic labor, sexual abuse, and abortion when pregnancy resulted.[37] In a lengthy investigation into the Southern Baptist Convention, the denomination was found guilty of covering up pervasive clergy sexual abuse of women and minors.[38] Willow Creek Community Church is another example of a church that turned out to have rampant abuse, with women suffering for several decades under the predations of the head pastor and another male.[39]

36. Ruth Graham, "What the Latest Investigations into the Catholic Church Sex Abuse Mean," *New York Times*, June 2, 2023, https://www.nytimes.com /2023/06/02/us/catholic-church-sex-abuse-investigations.html.
37. "Vatican Magazine Denounces Sexual Abuse of Nuns by Priests," *Irish Examiner*, February 1, 2019, https://www.irishexaminer.com/world/arid-30901659 .html; "Pope Admits Clerical Abuse of Nuns Including Sexual Slavery," *BBC*, February 6, 2019, https://www.bbc.com/news/world-europe-47134033.
38. *The Southern Baptist Convention Executive Committee's Response to Sexual Abuse Allegations and an Audit of the Procedures and Actions of the Credentials Committee* (Guidepost Solutions, May 15, 2022), available at https:// www.documentcloud.org/documents/22028383-guidepost-investigation-of-the -southern-baptist-convention/, p. 3.
39. Kelsey Hanson Woodruff, "A Calculated Attack on Clergy Abuse: Challenging Patriarchal Power at Willow Creek Community Church," *Theology and Sexuality* 30, no. 1 (2024): 35–36, 44.

In all three cases—the Catholic church, the Southern Baptist Convention, and Willow Creek Community Church—the organizations were shown to have covered up the abuse, protected abusers, and disbelieved those reporting the abuse. Willow Creek is egalitarian, and the Southern Baptist Convention and the Roman Catholic Church are complementarian, yet the abuse within all three is similar. Men held more organizational power and were able to use that power to their own advantage. Power centralized in the hands of one group (male clergy) over others (children, women, laypersons) contributed to the problem, resulting in what I have elsewhere called "institutional assault." Institutional assault occurs when "powerful organizations assault women by condoning sexual harassment and abuse, silencing victims, and vilifying those who report it."[40] That pattern played out in all three institutions.[41]

Power can also be abused at an individual level, as happened to Ruth Tucker. A respected author and professor, she was married for many years to a pastor who abused her violently. His justification was Bible verses that he claimed made him the leader and obligated her, as his wife, to submit to him in everything, including physical and sexual assault.[42] Dr. Tucker

40. Amy B. Diehl and Leanne M. Dzubinski, *Glass Walls: Shattering the Six Gender Bias Barriers That Still Hold Women Back at Work* (Rowman & Littlefield, 2023), 146.

41. Additional Christian organizations guilty of institutional assault would be Liberty University (Elissa Nadworny, "Liberty University Fined $14 Million for Federal Crime Reporting Violations," NPR, March 5, 2024, https://www.npr.org/2024/03/05/1236019397/liberty-university-clery-act-safety-crime) and Ravi Zacharias Ministries (Lynsey M. Barron and William P. Eiselstein, *Report of Independent Investigations into Sexual Misconduct of Ravi Zacharias* [Miller & Martin, PLLC, 2021], https://www.courthousenews.com/wp-content/uploads/2021/02/zacharias-report.pdf). The problem is not just a few bad actors; instead, it is a structural problem in Christian organizations.

42. Ruth A. Tucker, *Black and White Bible, Black and Blue Wife: My Story of Finding Hope After Domestic Abuse* (Zondervan, 2016), 132. While Ruth Tucker's story of her years of abuse is horrifying, she did escape and find health

is certainly not the only woman to suffer abuse at the hands of a man wielding Bible verses in his defense; she was willing to make her story public to aid other women caught in similar situations. According to the National Coalition Against Domestic Violence, one in four women experiences some form of intimate partner violence in her life.[43] Globally, the numbers are closer to one in three women.[44] Many of those women may be sitting in church pews on Sunday mornings.

The point of this section is not that any man with power over a woman will surely abuse it, but that a system that grants power to one group (men) over another group (women) and calls that structure God's will inherently creates challenges for women's flourishing and, worse, is easily abused. In fact, a recent study by Andrew Bauman with 2,800 women who work in the church found that church is not necessarily a safe place for women. Consider these statistics: 82 percent said sexism plays a role in church; 78 percent said their ministry has been limited because of their gender; 62 percent are not surprised at hearing sexist jokes at church; and 35 percent have experienced sexual assault or misconduct at church.[45] Read those statistics again. The problems I have been discussing in this book are not one-offs or exceptions to the norm; they are the standard experiences of many—or most—women in Christian organizations.

---

and healing. Her book does an excellent job of showing the difference between a healthy marriage between equal partners and the dangers inherent in unequal partnerships where the man is vested with final authority.

43. "Domestic Violence," National Coalition Against Domestic Violence, accessed April 3, 2025, https://assets.speakcdn.com/assets/2497/domestic_violence-2020080709350855.pdf?1596828650457,%20https://bjs.ojp.gov/female-murder-victims-and-victim-offender-relationship-2021.

44. "Facts and Figures: Ending Violence Against Women," UN Women, November 25, 2024, https://www.unwomen.org/en/articles/facts-and-figures/facts-and-figures-ending-violence-against-women.

45. Andrew J. Bauman, "Is the Church a Safe Place for Women?," *CBE International*, January 23, 2025, https://www.cbeinternational.org/resource/is-the-church-a-safe-place-for-women/.

These are problems that churches and Christian organizations cannot afford to ignore.

Genderwashing

Genderwashing is a term used to describe the gap between an organization's statements and its practices regarding gender. Wendy Fox-Kirk and her colleagues define the term this way: "Genderwashing is the process whereby organizational rhetoric about equality differs from the lived experiences of marginalized workers, creating the myth of gender equality while individuals in the organization continue to experience persistent gender discrimination due to organizational structure and cultural practices such as policies, procedures, and norms."[46] Genderwashing happens when there is a gap between an organization's stated values and its actual practices.

Gaps between beliefs and practices are not uncommon. Chris Argyris describes these gaps: "Human beings manifest two kinds of theories of action. One that they espouse and the second that they actually use (theory-in-use)."[47] Since Argyris named the gap between espoused theories and theories-in-use, a host of research has been done to understand and find ways to close such gaps. Moreover, the idea that humans have a gap between what they say they believe and value and what they actually *do* is familiar to most Christians. The apostle Paul lamented in Romans 7:15, "I do not understand my own actions. For I do not do what I want, but I do the very thing I hate." He is grieving over the gap.

In organizations with a complementarian theology that calls women "equal in value but different in role," the gap that

46. Wendy Fox-Kirk et al., "Genderwashing: The Myth of Equality," *Human Resource Development International* 23, no. 5 (2020): 588.

47. Chris Argyris, "Unrecognized Defenses of Scholars: Impact on Theory and Research," *Organization Science* 7, no. 1 (1996): 79.

creates genderwashing is easy to see.[48] The required role differences function as policies that discriminate against women
based solely on their gender. More difficult situations occur in
egalitarian organizations that affirm women's equality without
changing the organizational culture, structures, and practices
to align with their values.

Willow Creek Church is an example of what can happen
when an egalitarian organization has a gap between its theology
and its practice. Although the church claimed a strong egalitarian theology and had women on its pastoral staff for years,
nevertheless two leading champions of egalitarian theology
spent decades abusing women. Kelsey Woodruff explains that
the official egalitarian theological position operated in a culture
of patriarchy, privileging men over women and creating systems and structures where the abuse could continue unhindered;
when it was reported, it was initially contested as attacks and
lies. It took public pressure from journalists for the truth of the
abuse to finally become public.[49] Woodruff explains, "Evangelical churches like Willow Creek that hold to an egalitarian polity
are unable to enact gender equity for two reasons: (1) Naturalized patriarchy that is imported from greater American culture
and from complementarian evangelical spaces through cultural
products and discourse, and (2) gender individualism that prevents gender solidarity and structural transformation."[50] The
naturalized patriarchy that she describes is reflected in the social and Christian gender roles being discussed in this chapter.
Gender individualism describes the belief that gender is an
individual choice rather than something created through social mores as described in the section on gender essentialist

48. The "equal but different" language is a staple of complementarian theology.
See Grudem, "Letter from Wayne Grudem."
49. Woodruff, "Calculated Attack on Clergy Abuse," 35.
50. Woodruff, "Calculated Attack on Clergy Abuse," 37.

thinking in chapter 3. The two ways of thinking combine to make achieving egalitarian practice challenging.

In the context of Christian organizations, this gap between what people say they believe and what actually happens can be highly damaging to women. Statements of women's value and equality coupled with practices that marginalize, exclude, communicate less value, and even allow for abuse create cognitive dissonance for women. Such experiences are a form of gaslighting. Women who see the gap may depart, taking their energy and talents to places willing to value them.[51] Given the hypocrisy inherent in genderwashing, it is no wonder women leave.[52]

Christian organizations would do well to take seriously the consequences of gender role stereotypes. The perpetuation of prejudiced views of women, the very real potential for abuses of power, and the disconnect created by a gap between stated values and actual practices have very real consequences. In addition, these stereotypes are not aligned with biblical teaching, as I discuss next.

Scripture's Perspective

In this section I will look at what the Bible has to say on the topics discussed in this chapter. The qualities stereotypically

---

51. Gender bias at work has been connected to turnover intent (Eden B. King et al., "Understanding Tokenism: Antecedents and Consequences of a Psychological Climate of Gender Inequity," *Journal of Management* 36, no. 2 [2010]: 503), as has male-normed organizational culture (Amy B. Diehl et al., "Measuring the Invisible: Development and Multi-Industry Validation of the Gender Bias Scale for Women Leaders," *Human Resource Development Quarterly* 31, no. 3 [2020]: 270).

52. Recent studies show more women than men leaving the church. See Daniel A. Cox and Kelsey Eyre Hammond, "Young Women Are Leaving Church in Unprecedented Numbers," Survey Center on American Life, April 4, 2024, https://www.americansurveycenter.org/newsletter/young-women-are-leaving-church-in-unprecedented-numbers/. The authors explain that nearly two-thirds of Gen Z women don't think churches treat men and women equally. These women are not wrong, as this book shows.

ascribed to women are not, in themselves, problematic. The problem is when such behaviors and attitudes are expected of women in ways they are not expected of men, and when women are penalized in ways men are not if they do not exhibit these behaviors. Yet all too often that happens. As Adam Grant explains, "A man who doesn't help is 'busy,' a woman is 'selfish.'"[53] The exact same behavior is characterized differently based on who is being evaluated. But that approach is cultural, not scriptural. In reality, the Bible establishes identical standards for men and for women.

Chapter 3 showed that spiritual gifts are not distributed based on gender, nor are virtues and vices gendered. This chapter builds on those ideas by looking at what the Bible has to say about how Christians interact with one another. The characteristics expected of Christians toward one another are love and service. Christians—all Christians, not just women—are called to die to self in support of one another. Women are men's *ezer kenegdo* (strong ally), not their subordinate helpers.[54] These concepts offer a needed corrective to gender role stereotypes.

Love and Serve One Another

Shortly before his betrayal, Jesus gave his followers these instructions: "I give you a new commandment, that you love one another. Just as I have loved you, you also should love one another. By this everyone will know that you are my disciples, if you have love for one another" (John 13:34–35). Women who are supportive of others, put others first, or prioritize others' needs ahead of their own are showing love to others. And such

---

53. Adam Grant, "Are You Selfish or Just Busy? It Depends on Your Gender," *The Next Big Idea Club*, April 8, 2016, https://nextbigideaclub.com/magazine /adam-grant-selfish-just-busy-depends-gender/7361/. Note that being busy is socially acceptable, whereas being "selfish" is prohibited in Phil. 2:3: "Do nothing from selfish ambition."
54. *Ezer kenegdo* is discussed in more detail in a following section.

expectations are routinely placed on women in ways they are not placed on men. Yet Jesus's instructions are not addressed exclusively to women; instead, they are addressed to all his followers.

Jesus also encouraged his followers to serve one another rather than exercising power over each other: "But Jesus called them to him and said, 'You know that the rulers of the gentiles lord it over them, and their great ones are tyrants over them. It will not be so among you, but whoever wishes to be great among you must be your servant, and whoever wishes to be first among you must be your slave, just as the Son of Man came not to be served but to serve and to give his life a ransom for many'" (Matt. 20:25–28). Jesus voluntarily laid down his power as God, and he calls all his followers to voluntarily lay down their power.

Paul also taught love and service. He encouraged the Roman church this way: "Be devoted to one another in love. Honor one another above yourselves" (Rom. 12:10 NIV). And in writing to the Galatian church, Paul tells them "through love become enslaved to one another. For the whole law is summed up in a single commandment, 'You shall love your neighbor as yourself'" (Gal. 5:13b–14).

Current organizational structures and practices virtually always give men more power than women. Jesus's command is to break that cycle and for those with power to use that power for the good of others. Paul's instructions are for followers of Jesus to serve and love others, caring for them the same way one does for oneself. In many ways men can live out these commands by laying down their social power for the good of their women colleagues.

Die to Self

Another scriptural example of how those with power should treat those with less power can be seen in Philippians. Paul exhorts the believers in Philippi with these words:

Do nothing from selfish ambition or empty conceit, but in humility regard others as better than yourselves. Let each of you look not to your own interests but to the interests of others. Let the same mind be in you that was in Christ Jesus,

> who, though he existed in the form of God,
> > did not regard equality with God
> > as something to be grasped,
> but emptied himself,
> > taking the form of a slave,
> > assuming human likeness.
> And being found in appearance as a human,
> > he humbled himself
> > and became obedient to the point of death—
> > even death on a cross. (Phil. 2:3–8)

Paul's standard for how believers are to treat one another is the pinnacle of self-sacrifice, what Jesus did for humans. Yet somehow, in much Christian thinking, women are the ones expected to sacrifice their own self-interest for the good of their families. Men may be given a pass on daily sacrifice, told their self-sacrifice is only needed in times of extreme physical danger. Yet such a message does not reflect biblical teaching; it is an inadequate portrayal of Christian values.[55]

Women as Ezer Kenegdo

In Genesis 1 God says seven times that something is good (Gen. 1:4, 10, 12, 18, 21, 25, 31). So the statement in Genesis 2:18 that something is "not good" is jarring. God says it is not good for the man to be alone. Cultural thinking has popularized the idea that what the man needs is support (and sex), and Bible translations of *ezer kenegdo* as "helper" or "help

---

55. Hollywood's Westerns, hero, and action movies have done a lot to create this social expectation for men.

meet" have contributed to the idea of women as subordinate assistants to men.[56]

But a close look at the text suggests that what the man actually needs is an ally. He needs someone just like him who is on his side and who will be hand in hand with him throughout his life. The phrase *ezer kenegdo* describes that kind of relationship.[57] The word *ezer* occurs twenty-one times in the Old Testament.[58] Of those, sixteen of them are used to describe God as Israel's help, strength, and defense. The word is decidedly military, indicating a warrior, not someone in a subordinate position. Similarly, *kenegdo* is best translated as "corresponding," making the whole phrase "a saving strength corresponding to him."[59] What Adam needs is not a servant; he needs a partner-ally to work the garden and populate the earth with him.

Chapter 3 looked at the Proverbs 31 woman and Abigail as examples of strong women managers. They and other women in Scripture exhibit the attributes stereotypically assigned to men. Abigail took charge in a life-and-death situation to save her household from destruction (1 Sam. 25:18–34). Shiphrah and Puah, the Hebrew midwives, took charge by defying Pharaoh's order to kill baby boys (Exod. 1:15–21). Rahab hid the Israelite spies in direct contradiction to her king's orders (Josh. 2). Deborah led Israel, made decisions regarding disputes, and directed the commander of the Israelite army how to fight against the Canaanites (Judg. 4:4–7). In that fight, Jael was the one who took decisive action and killed the leader of the Canaanite army (Judg. 4:17–22). Each of these women showed leadership, decisiveness, independence, and initiative: in short,

---

56. The ESV, NASB, and NIV all use "helper" for the woman. The KVJ, ASV, and Geneva Bible all say "help meet."

57. Tucker, *Black and White Bible*, 34.

58. Exod. 18:4; Deut. 33:7, 26, 29; Pss. 20:2; 33:20; 70:5; 89:19; 115:9, 10, 11; 121:1, 2; 124:8; 146:5; Isa. 30:5; Ezek. 12:14; Dan. 11:34; Hosea 13:9.

59. Payne, *The Bible vs. Biblical Womanhood*, 4.

the agentic qualities that society and some Christian thinking reserve for men. In doing so they fulfilled the *ezer kenegdo* role God planned all along.

In conclusion, there is nothing in the Bible to support the gender role stereotypes presented in this chapter. And there is plenty of teaching in the Bible that works to counter these stereotypes, allowing women and men to flourish as full humans. Finally, biblical texts are also clear in their calls for humility and freely shared power among followers of Jesus.

Strategies to See Women as Leaders

The strategies needed to address the challenges described in this chapter are perhaps some of the most difficult, yet the most Christlike, of every problem discussed so far, because the solutions to these problems require those with more power— men—to effectively die to self as Jesus did and as Paul described in Philippians 2. Only by recognizing and then willingly laying down some of their own privileges, powers, and rights can men begin to create spaces where women can truly flourish as full humans made in the image of God.

This is another area where surface strategies are straightforward, but deeper work will be needed to change fundamental thinking. The stereotypes presented in this chapter, the ones that have been labeled biblical womanhood and biblical manhood, are not from Scripture. They come from culture and reflect the same gender essentialist views discussed in chapter 3. But attitudes can be changed, and the benefits to all members of an organization will be worth the effort.

I will start with some of the easier strategies to begin changing workplace practices. Learning about stereotypes, using the "flip it to test it" strategy, encouraging and negotiating with a woman you'd like to see in a leadership role, and promoting nuanced views of good leadership are excellent places to start.

Learn About Stereotypes

First, learn about these (and other) stereotypes that society and organizations apply when thinking about people. Become so familiar with them that you notice immediately when someone makes a statement attributing stereotypical qualities to a woman. Be vigilant for racialized stereotypes as well. When you hear such language, consider whether the comment is actually true of a particular woman, simply an assumption, or worse, an unspoken expectation. Married leaders also need to consider how they talk about their own wives and families. Are you communicating, unintentionally or not, that you view women as only belonging in the home and caring for family?

Use the "Flip It to Test It" Strategy

If you are not sure about a comment, "Flip it to test it."[60] Try turning the comment around to see if you would say it the other way. For example, if someone says, "We can't promote Carla because she's emotional," ask if you would make the same comment about Carlos. If not, the statement is likely based on a stereotype or is wrongly applying a stereotypical belief to a woman.

Encourage and Negotiate

If you invite a woman to a leadership role and she is hesitant or turns it down, probe a bit. Be curious. Ask questions. What is behind her refusal? Is she worried about extra hours? Managing the workload? Needing flexibility for caretaking responsibilities? Thinking she will not be supported and taken seriously? See if some encouragement and negotiation will enable her to say yes to the opportunity. Similarly, ask yourself if the opportunity was clearly explained and if you showed her why she is a good fit for the role. Remember that women may believe

60. See https://flipittotestit.com.

they need complete competence before they take something on. Explain how she will be mentored and trained for the new responsibilities. If you believe she is a good fit, help her see that too and provide the support she needs to do the job.

Promote Nuanced Views of Good Leadership

Plenty of research shows that good leaders use both agentic and communal qualities. In fact, the earliest studies that identified these two sets of qualities needed by leaders were done in the 1950s just with men.[61] The bifurcation of some qualities as "masculine" and others as "feminine" was not part of the original work because men were assumed to be able to provide both. Since then, research continues to show that achieving tasks and caring for people are the core functions of leadership.[62] Research also continues to show that leadership teams with a diversity of voices and perspectives perform better.[63] So not only

61. These early studies were conducted by The Ohio State University and the University of Michigan and were done with railroad managers and other managers. See Daniel Katz, Nathan Maccoby, and Nancy C. Morse, *Productivity, Supervision and Morale in an Office Situation* (University of Michigan, 1950); Katz et al., *Productivity, Supervision and Morale Among Railroad Workers*; Stogdill and Coons, *Leader Behavior*; Peter Weissenberg and Michael J. Kavanagh, "The Independence of Initiating Structure and Consideration: A Review of the Evidence," *Personnel Psychology* 25, no. 1 (1972): 119–30.

62. For example, Peter Northouse's classic definition of leadership is: "Leadership is a process whereby an individual influences a group of individuals to achieve a common goal" (Peter G. Northouse, *Leadership: Theory and Practice*, 8th ed. [SAGE, 2019], 5). While the individualistic focus and unidirectional nature have been contested, the core points of working with people and getting something done still matter.

63. For example, diverse teams are more innovative (see Rachel D. Godsil et al., *The Science of Equality*, vol. 2, *The Effects of Gender Roles, Implicit Bias, and Stereotype Threat on the Lives of Women and Girls* [Perception Institute, 2016], 55). Organizations with diverse teams also perform better financially (see Marcus Noland, Tyler Moran, and Barbara Kotschwar, *Is Gender Diversity Profitable? Evidence from A Global Survey* [Peterson Institute for International Economics, 2016], https://www.piie.com/publications/working-papers/gender-diversity-profitable -evidence-global-survey) and are less likely to be found guilty of misconduct (Francesca Arnaboldi et al., "Gender Diversity and Bank Misconduct," *Journal of Corporate Finance* 71 [2021], https://doi.org/10.1016/j.jcorpfin.2020.101834).

is reducing barriers to women's organizational leadership the right thing to do, but it is likely to benefit the organization.[64] Changing the organization's perspective on what makes a good leader will be worth the work involved.

Study What the Bible Says About Humility and Power

Do a Bible study or sermon series on Christian virtues such as humility and on Jesus's teachings on power. Emphasize that these teachings apply at work every bit as much as anywhere else. And emphasize the need for those with more social and organizational power—men—to use that power for the good of others, and to give up that power in service of their women colleagues.

Another Bible study could focus on characteristics of followers of Jesus, emphasizing that these same qualities are for everyone, not some for women and others for men. Help people distinguish between what culture teaches and what the Bible actually says.

Learn How to Be an Ally

The concept of allies is worth considering here. When God created Adam and Eve, he put them in the garden as allies, to work with and support one another. The consequences of the

64. In December of 2024 Costco's shareholders requested that the company back away from DEI initiatives and eliminate the Chief Diversity Officer position. The Costco board's answer was a clear "no." Their reasoning was clear: The move would not help shareholders, and maintaining DEI values "enables us to attract and retain employees who will help our business succeed. . . . Serving [our members] with a diverse group of employees enhances satisfaction. . . . Members like to see themselves reflected in the people in our warehouses with whom they interact. . . . [Diversity] fosters creativity and innovation in the merchandise and services that we offer our members" (Doug Melville, "Costco Doubled Down on DEI as a Business Case: What We Can All Learn," *Forbes*, December 30, 2024, https://www.forbes.com/sites/dougmelville/2024/12/30/costco-doubled-down-on -dei-as-a-business-case-what-we-can-all-learn/). For Costco, the business case for diversity is compelling.

fall have been to pit women and men against one another, rupturing the "good" that God intended and reinforcing the "not good" of men being alone. The concept of allies has become an excellent way of describing, in secular terms, the actions of those with more social power in supporting those with less social power. An ally can be anyone who supports another, and it has become common to speak of male allies for women and white allies for people of color. Yet at the core, the concept of an ally is distinctly Christian. Jesus was humanity's greatest "ally" in that he laid down not just his power but his life on our behalf. In doing so he set the example that Christians also should be allies for those with less power. When Ruth Tucker eventually reported her situation to the seminary president, his response was full allyship: "Why haven't you come to me earlier? . . . Are you okay? Do you have a support network . . . ? How is your son doing? Of course you're doing the right thing to escape with your son."[65] What an excellent model of allyship.

Chapter Summary

This chapter has looked at the pressing problem of social gender role stereotypes that were then merged with Christianity and proclaimed as Christian gender roles. Nevertheless, these roles as requirements for men and women have no basis in biblical teaching but are completely cultural. Next, the chapter discussed how Scripture offers different, healthier ways of viewing men and women. Loving and serving one another, dying to self, and seeing women as men's "strong ally" rather than subordinate helper are good correctives to faulty cultural thinking about women. Finally, the chapter offered some practical strategies to help leaders and male colleagues become better allies for the women around them.

65. Tucker, *Black and White Bible*, 11.

Conclusion

Some Final Questions and an Invitation

n this book I have presented and analyzed five key issues that hinder women from flourishing at work in Christian organizations. The first issue was an overemphasis on sex, where women are seen primarily as sexualized beings and therefore threatening to men's virtue. The second issue was one of language: I considered the way masculine language and speaking patterns marginalize women and make it difficult for them to contribute and flourish. The third issue was the complex constellation of beliefs about work and workplace culture that makes it virtually impossible for women to flourish. The fourth issue was the persistent attitude of ambivalence toward women, seen when others doubt their competence and their qualifications. The final issue was the difficulty of seeing women as capable of leading due to the strength of gender role stereotypes embedded in Christian thinking. These challenges are not unique to Christian organizations, but they seem more pronounced in Christian settings than secular ones because of the ways they have been tied to theology and embedded into Christian faith, as I have shown.

In this conclusion I will discuss some final questions to help organizational leaders, members, and individual women better understand these patterns and find new ways to think about them. First, I ask what it means to be truly countercultural. Next, I ask why Christians so quickly follow culture even when they do not intend to do so. Third, I address what I believe to be the core problem underlying all these issues. Finally, I consider the insufficiency of egalitarian theology alone to address these problems. The chapter closes with an invitation to leaders, organizational allies, and women to imagine and move toward a healthier future for everyone.

What Does It Mean to Be Countercultural?

Christians often talk about wanting to be countercultural; that is seen as a high value. After all, Romans 12:2 commands believers, "Do not be conformed to this age, but be transformed by the renewing of the mind, so that you may discern what is the will of God—what is good and acceptable and perfect." And Jesus clearly went against the cultural norms of his own day. Consider, for example, the three pericopes in Mark 10: Jesus disputes the disciples' understanding of a man's right to divorce his wife; welcomes the children seeking him, whom the disciples wanted to block; and explains to the disciples that wealth will not bring someone into God's kingdom. In all three cases the disciples seem perplexed. Their culture had taught them to see things one way, and Jesus saw things completely differently.

Much of the work in this book has shown how Christian thinking on women has been deeply influenced by culture. Sometimes people simply read their own culture into Scripture. Sometimes people argue that cultures of a previous day were more aligned with Scripture, and thus they call for a return to those values that they imagine to have been better.[1] What this book has tried to show is that, when it comes to women, the starting values have virtually always been cultural. And sadly, some of those cultural values are easily found in Scripture because it was also written in patriarchal societies and described similar situations for women. But we must not confuse describing how things are with prescribing how things should be.[2] For example, Christian proponents of slavery made that mistake by arguing that since slavery was described in the Bible, it was therefore part of God's plan. Similarly, descriptions of women in ancient cultures as subordinate to men and being practically property, belonging to fathers, husbands, and sons, soon became treated as prescriptions of how God intended things to be.[3]

While I value the call for Christians to be countercultural, in this book I have taken a different approach to getting there. I have taken a deep and serious look at research into American culture to understand what is going on for women. Then I placed these cultural beliefs and practices under the microscope of Scripture, to see to what degree they align with God's plans for God's people. And in many cases the answer has been that what American culture—and American evangelical subculture

1. I say "imagine to have been better" because the reality is that these values likely were not better, or were only selectively better. See Stephanie Coontz, *The Way We Never Were: American Families and the Nostalgia Trap* (Basic Books, 1992). Coontz unpacks the reality behind nostalgic ideas of the past.

2. For an excellent discussion of how culture operates in the biblical text, see William J. Webb, *Slaves, Women and Homosexuals: Exploring the Hermeneutics of Cultural Analysis* (IVP Academic, 2001), 21–29.

3. William Webb discusses the problem with what he calls a "static hermeneutic," which he describes as "primarily interested in exegeting the text as an isolated entity and finding comparable or equivalent expressions . . . of how that text may be lived out in another culture." He points out that treating the slavery texts in Scripture as useful for today's employer/employee relationship breaks down in the face of texts such as Peter telling slaves to accept beatings for the sake of the gospel, or Old Testament law that prescribed lesser penalties for the rape of a slave than of a free woman. Webb, *Slaves, Women and Homosexuals*, 36–37.

too—creates and promotes for women looks nothing like what God wants.

Why Is Culture's Influence So Strong?

If culture's plans for women and God's plans for women are different, as I have argued in this book, that leads to the question of why so many in the Christian faith think otherwise. Or more plainly stated, Why have Christians so closely followed culture in deciding how to think about women? The answer, at least in part, is that humans have all been socialized into the same patriarchal system, and it is very difficult to see one's own culture clearly. Like the proverbial fish that cannot see the water in which it swims, humans are not good at clearly seeing the culture in which we operate. In this day and age, it is relatively easy to gain exposure to another culture; that exposure can begin to make people aware of different value systems. However, it requires more than just exposure to truly put competing values and views into dialogue with one another and arrive at a more considered perspective. I have attempted some of that work in the preceding chapters.

Additionally, the Bible itself is the product of a variety of times and cultures, reflecting the practices and values of those times and places.[4] When we lack familiarity with and intimate knowledge of those times and cultures, it becomes more challenging to understand the scriptural record. In an area such as the treatment of women, the challenge is great. US culture is still heavily patriarchal, and women are still relatively less powerful than men, just as was true in the times when the Bible was written. The disparities today are fewer than in Bible times, but they still exist. And patriarchal beliefs about women, though less strong now than in much of the Bible, still persist. Therefore, it becomes much more difficult to separate culture from Scripture,

---

4. Webb, *Slaves, Women and Homosexuals*, 22–24.

and it is easier to mistakenly see overlap between what today's culture practices and what the biblical text describes. And so, many of today's Christians continue to proclaim as scriptural things that, when carefully examined, may have described how things were in that time but are not meant as a guide to how things should be today.

What Is the Core Challenge?

At its root, the core problem underlying the issues discussed in this book is one of not valuing women the way God does. The view of women as less valuable than men came about after sin entered the world and is the product of centuries of cultural views that have not aligned with biblical teaching. Scripture from start to finish teaches that women are of just as much value as men. Still, the norm in too many Christian organizations has been and continues to be to see women as less valuable. Even in organizations that make clear statements about women's value and worth, practices too often still default to those that favor men, as this book has shown.

And that lack of value has enormous consequences: consequences for women, for men, and for organizations, societies, and cultures. Paul, in describing Christians as members of Christ's body, states: "If one member suffers, all suffer together with it" (1 Cor. 12:26). How much greater are the consequences if half the members suffer! As Carolyn James explains, "Health is a whole body concern that is jeopardized if any organ or limb is weak or not functioning properly. The person who has one strong leg and one that is weak is not viewed as strong because they have a strong leg. To the contrary, they are lame and in need of physical therapy to restore the weak leg to full strength."[5] When half or more of the followers of Jesus suffer

5. Carolyn Custis James, *When Life and Beliefs Collide: How Knowing God Makes a Difference* (Zondervan, 2001), 205.

from being undervalued, then the entire church and the entire Christian organization is depleted. James continues, "If this biblical imagery of the body means anything, the church cannot reach maturity so long as women are marginalized."[6] The church is not the only organization impacted either. Any Christian organization—nonprofit, mission agency, educational institution—seeking to serve God will not be able to do its best work when women are not fully valued. In short, when women are undervalued, God's work in the world is hampered.

At its root, the solution to this problem is quite simple: valuing women the way God does. True valuing goes far beyond statements of equal worth, or positive statements about women. True valuing must be lived out in practice. There must be evidence, as the book of James says: "But someone will say, 'You have faith, and I have works.' Show me your faith apart from works, and I by my works will show you faith" (2:18). Just as the fruit of faith is evident, so is the fruit of valuing women. Each chapter has suggested concrete practices and attitudes that will show women that they are fully valued. When women are fully valued, they will flourish and so will their organizations.

Doesn't Egalitarian Theology Solve the Problem?

An important question to consider is whether an egalitarian theology is sufficient to counteract or eliminate the problems presented in this book. If your organization holds an egalitarian theology, you may think that your work is done and the problems are solved. But even in churches and organizations with sound egalitarian theology, organizational systems and practices almost certainly still favor men over women. There is a gap between the stated values (espoused values) and the practice

6. James, *When Life and Beliefs Collide*, 206.

(values in use).[7] That gap between egalitarian theology and equitable organizational practices is created by patriarchal norms.

For Christian organizations, there are at least two reasons for this gap between the espoused values and the values in use. First are the centuries of Christian thinking and practice that have been constructed in patriarchal societies reflecting patriarchal norms. Second, the wider culture in which Christian organizations operate is still strongly patriarchal. So Christian organizations have absorbed patriarchal practices both from their own history and from the societies around them. They may be so steeped in these cultural norms that they cannot even see the inconsistencies. That is part of the challenge of culture already discussed in this chapter.

Organizations that hold an egalitarian value system are at particular risk of becoming guilty of genderwashing, as described in chapter 5. Genderwashing happens when the outward face of an organization is egalitarian. Public documents, statements, and outward-facing practices may state that men and women are equal. Yet internal practices continue to prefer men over women, and the conditions inside the organization are not markedly better than those in any other organization. Organizations with egalitarian theology must be the first to examine—and correct—systems and structures that disadvantage women. In this book I have examined and unpacked five such areas, providing ways to begin and follow through with the needed changes so all organizational members can flourish.

An Invitation

In this final section of the book, I want to issue some invitations. First are invitations to leaders, to lead the way in bringing

7. Chris Argyris, "Unrecognized Defenses of Scholars: Impact on Theory and Research," *Organization Science* 7, no. 1 (1996): 79. See chap. 5 for more on the challenges for organizations with egalitarian theology.

organizational change. Second are invitations to allies, to support your women colleagues in their work and your leaders in bringing change. Last are invitations to women, to learn about how gender operates at work and perhaps clarify your own experiences, in a way that enables you to continue to grow and serve in healthy ways.

An Invitation to Leaders

If you are an organizational leader reading this book, first of all, thank you! I appreciate your investment of time and energy to learn about these issues. I hope this book has enabled you to see, perhaps in a new way, some of the ways men are accorded higher status and privilege by society. And I hope it has reminded you that God expects those with higher status and privilege to leverage that privilege for the benefit of others. Last, I hope you have seen that benefiting women will benefit your organization. Rather than being a zero-sum game, where in order for one to win another must lose, strengthening women in your organization is an all-around win. Women are free to be their best selves and bring their full talents to the workplace. When women thrive, the whole organization benefits.

I hope this book has given you practical insight into ways to support women and therefore all members of your organization. I invite you to share what you have learned. Take the initiative and the responsibility to work for change. Take the initiative to learn more, to read more, and to become more familiar with what it is like for Christian women to work in a Christian organization.

I also invite you to explore the specific experiences of women in your own organization. Beyond the general knowledge you can gain from reading and educating yourself, find out exactly what women in your church or school or nonprofit experience. Invite them to share what is working for them and what pain points they encounter. Simple conversations and an open ear to listen can help you understand what is happening. For a deeper diagnosis, consider using the Gender Bias Scale for Women Leaders as a tool.[8] The survey will enable women in your organization to point out what they experience and allow you to pick an area in which to begin the change process. The primary responsibility lies with you as the organizational leader. You are the one with the power to create change and the authority to make it happen. So get started! Pick one area and work on it, then another. You may be pleasantly surprised at how quickly things improve once you get going.

An Invitation to Allies

If you are an ally reading this book, first of all, thank you! I appreciate your investment of time and energy to learn about these issues. The ally role is critically important. You can serve as a mediator between women who are frustrated by their experiences and male leaders who do not understand the issues. You can serve as an advocate for those with less power to those with more power. You can serve as an educator to bring greater awareness to members of your organization about the challenges women face and solutions to those challenges. All these roles are vital. In filling them, you live out what Jesus did for humanity.

I hope this book has given you insight into ways you can help support your women colleagues. I encourage you to keep learning. Do your own reading and research to understand what it is like for women generally and women in your organization. Then, I invite you to start sharing what you have learned with others. Build and grow the ally network in your organization. Perhaps what you have learned here can be applied in more than one setting, for example, at work and at church.

8. Amy B. Diehl et al., "Measuring the Invisible: Development and Multi-Industry Validation of the Gender Bias Scale for Women Leaders," *Human Resource Development Quarterly* 31, no. 3 (2020): 249–80.

I invite you to continue the needed work of speaking up and speaking out for those who could benefit from an additional voice in their corner. Thank you for your allyship!

An Invitation to Women

If you are a woman reading this book, I also thank you. And I suspect that little here has surprised you. As I have said elsewhere, the primary responsibility for organizational change lies with leaders.[9] Yet women can also contribute to the path for change and improvement. You too can start by learning about the challenges. Learn to name and recognize the issues presented in this book and in other resources. Understanding the challenges can help you not take things personally but realize these are system issues. Recognizing what is impacting you can also help you make strategic decisions. Maybe you can strengthen relationships with other women and with allies at work. Maybe you can launch a book club to continue educating yourself and others about these challenges. Christian women are often strongly socialized to be nice and to be submissive, so learning about these issues and speaking up about them may feel very risky. Yet some risk is necessary if change is going to happen. Learning may also feel empowering, helping you see the challenges that are built into organizations and that get in the way of you doing your best work. Learning may also help clarify some of your experiences and give you those "aha moments" when something that previously just felt uncomfortable or off now makes sense. It may even help you discern when it is time to leave a toxic system that will not change.

I hope this book will embolden you to speak up and give you resources to help you when confronting unjust organizational practices. I invite you to share the book with others—both men

9. Amy B. Diehl and Leanne M. Dzubinski, *Glass Walls: Shattering the Six Gender Bias Barriers That Still Hold Women Back At Work* (Rowman & Littlefield, 2023), 194.

and women—who can help bring whatever change is needed in your organization. And share it with women, men, and leaders in your church and other organizations. Help Christian organizations become the "city built on a hill" showing everyone else the beauty of operating according to God's good plans.[10]

A Final Note

As I write these concluding lines, I am at a mission conference where the attendees are approximately 80 percent male. The conversations I hear are about "the missionary . . . he." And once again, I feel invisible. A few men have spoken with me; some will not even look at me. I do not know whether the problem is that they have a sexualized view of women, they think I do not belong here, they do not think I have anything to contribute, or they do not think a woman can lead in these circles. Yet the work they do in their respective locations undoubtedly includes women. Their organizations include women, and their constituencies include women. And I wonder how women can hear the good news of the gospel if the men in charge of the work do not even see the women in front of them.

At dinner my husband brought up the topic of how hard it is for women to be heard here. Another man did not want to believe that could be true. I affirmed that both research and my experience show it to be true. He was unhappily surprised and then he began to talk about the gender dynamics he had seen but not considered important. My hope is that just that small conversation made something visible to him that had been invisible before. And now that he can see it, he can do something about it.

---

10. See Matt. 5:14–16: "You are the light of the world. A city built on a hill cannot be hid. People do not light a lamp and put it under the bushel basket; rather, they put it on the lampstand, and it gives light to all in the house. In the same way, let your light shine before others, so that they may see your good works and give glory to your Father in heaven."

Being invisible is depressing, but the dinner conversation gives me hope. Followers of Jesus can do better than the rest of the world. Followers of Jesus have the full resources of the Holy Spirit to help in this work. And as brothers and sisters in Christ, coheirs with Jesus and members of his body, Christians have all the reasons to press into this important work of restoration. I am convinced that Christian organizations can and should model for the rest of the world how men and women can flourish together. May we see it happen!

Bibliography

Acker, Joan. "Hierarchies, Jobs, Bodies: A Theory of Gendered Organizations." *Gender & Society* 4, no. 2 (1990): 139–58.

Amanor-Boadu, Vincent. "Empirical Evidence for the 'Great Resignation.'" *Monthly Labor Review*, U.S. Bureau of Labor Statistics, November 2022. https://www.bls.gov/opub/mlr/2022/article/empirical-evidence-for-the -great-resignation.htm.

Argyris, Chris. "Unrecognized Defenses of Scholars: Impact on Theory and Research." *Organization Science* 7, no. 1 (1996): 79–87.

Arnaboldi, Francesca, Barbara Casu, Angela Gallo, Elena Kalotychou, and Anna Sarkisyan. "Gender Diversity and Bank Misconduct." *Journal of Corporate Finance* 71 (2021). https://doi.org/10.1016/j.jcorpfin.2020 .101834.

Arterburn, Stephen, and Fred Stoeker. *Every Man's Battle: Winning the War on Sexual Temptation One Victory at a Time.* 20th anniversary ed. WaterBrook, 2020.

"Average Working Hours (Statistical Data 2025)." Clockify, accessed March 21, 2025. https://clockify.me/working-hours.

Barr, Beth Allison. *The Making of Biblical Womanhood: How the Subjugation of Women Became Gospel Truth.* Brazos, 2021.

———. "Why Do We Devalue Women's Work in Christian Institutions?" Substack, October 19, 2023. https://bethallisonbarr.substack.com/p/why -do-we-devalue-womens-work-in.

Barrero, Jose Maria, Nicholas Bloom, and Stephen J. Davis. "The Evolution of Work from Home." *Journal of Economic Perspectives* 37, no. 4 (2023): 1–28.

Barron, Lynsey M., and William P. Eiselstein. *Report of Independent Investigations into Sexual Misconduct of Ravi Zacharias.* Miller & Martin, PLLC, 2021. https://www.courthousenews.com/wp-content/uploads/2021/02/zacharias-report.pdf.

Bauman, Andrew J. "Is the Church a Safe Place for Women?" *CBE International*, January 23, 2025. https://www.cbeinternational.org/resource/is-the-church-a-safe-place-for-women/.

Bennett, Jessica. "How Not to Be 'Manterrupted' in Meetings." *Time*, January 20, 2015. https://time.com/3666135/sheryl-sandberg-talking-while-female-manterruptions/.

Bluedorn, John, Francesca Caselli, Niels-Jakob Hansen, Ippei Shibata, and Marina A. Tavares. "Gender and Employment in the COVID-19 Recession: Cross-Country Evidence on 'She-Cessions.'" *Labour Economics* 81 (2023): 1–10.

Bond, Kimberly. "Feeling Despondent at Work? Why 2025 Is Set to Be the Year of the 'Great Detachment.'" *Bazaar*, April 16, 2025. https://www.harpersbazaar.com/culture/a64502127/great-detachment-career-trend/.

Bondestam, Fredrik, and Maja Lundqvist. "Sexual Harassment in Higher Education—a Systematic Review." *European Journal of Higher Education* 10, no. 4 (2020): 397–419.

Brenner, O. C., Joseph Tomkiewicz, and Virginia Ellen Schein. "The Relationship Between Sex Role Stereotypes and Requisite Management Characteristics Revisited." *Academy of Management Journal* 32, no. 3 (1989): 662–69.

Burchielli, Rosaria, Timothy Bartram, and Rani Thanacoody. "Work-Family Balance or Greedy Organizations?" *Industrial Relations* 63, no. 1 (2008): 108–33.

Catalyst. *Women in the Workforce: United States.* 2022. https://www.catalyst.org/insights/2022/women-in-the-workforce-united-states.

Chikwe, Chidinma Favour, Nkechi Emmanuella Eneh, and Chidiogo Uzoamaka Akpuokwe. "Navigating the Double Bind: Strategies for Women Leaders in Overcoming Stereotypes and Leadership Biases." *GSC Advanced Research and Reviews* 18, no. 3 (2024): 159–72.

Clawson, Jeff, Pete Jordan, Megan Loumagne Ulishney, and Stan Rosenberg. *2021 Report on Diversity at CCCU Institutions.* SCIO, 2021. https://www.scio-uk.org/wp-content/uploads/2021/09/2021-Report-on-Diversity-at-CCCU-Institutions.pdf.

Cohick, Lynn H. "The 'Woman at the Well': Was the Samaritan Woman Really an Adulteress?" In *Vindicating the Vixens: Revisiting the Sexualized, Vilified, and Marginalized Women of the Bible*, edited by Sandra Glahn, 249–54. Kregel Academic, 2017.

Coontz, Stephanie. *The Way We Never Were: American Families and the Nostalgia Trap.* Basic Books, 1992.

Cooper, Marianne, and Priya Fielding-Singh. "Younger Women's Experiences Show Gender Equity at Work Isn't Inevitable." *Harvard Business Review*, November 1, 2024. https://hbr.org/2024/11/younger-womens-experiences -show-gender-equity-at-work-isnt-inevitable.

Coser, Lewis A. "Greedy Organizations." *European Journal of Sociology* 8, no. 2 (1967): 196–215.

Cox, Daniel A., and Kelsey Eyre Hammond. "Young Women Are Leaving Church in Unprecedented Numbers." Survey Center on American Life, April 4, 2024. https://www.americansurveycenter.org/newsletter/young -women-are-leaving-church-in-unprecedented-numbers/.

Crittenden, Ann. *If You've Raised Kids, You Can Manage Anything: Leadership Begins at Home.* Gotham Books, 2004.

Currie, Jan, Patricia Harris, and Bev Thiele. "Sacrifices in Greedy Universities: Are They Gendered?" *Gender and Education* 12, no. 3 (2000): 269–91.

Curry, Janel, and Amy Reynolds. *Missional Effectiveness: Achieving Institutional Goals and Mission.* Women in Leadership National Study. Gordon College, 2017. https://s3.us-east-2.amazonaws.com/missio-research -projects/Missional-Effectiveness-Women-in-Leadership-Executive -Summary.pdf.

Diehl, Amy. B. "'Guys' Is Not Gender-Neutral—Let's Stop Using It Like It Is." *Fast Company*, January 7, 2024. https://www.fastcompany.com/90629391 /guys-is-not-gender-neutral-lets-stop-using-it-like-it-is.

Diehl, Amy B., and Leanne M. Dzubinski. *Glass Walls: Shattering the Six Gender Bias Barriers That Still Hold Women Back at Work.* Rowman & Littlefield, 2023.

——— "Making the Invisible Visible: A Cross-Sector Analysis of Gender-Based Leadership Barriers." *Human Resource Development Quarterly* 27, no. 2 (2016): 181–206.

———. "We Need to Stop 'Untitling' and 'Uncredentialing' Professional Women." *Fast Company*, January 22, 2021. https://www.fastcom pany.com/90596628/we-need-to-stop-untitling-and-uncredentialing -professional-women.

———. "We Need to Talk About Using Pet Names for Women at Work." *Fast Company*, October 29, 2020. https://www.fastcompany.com/90569439 /we-need-to-talk-about-using-pet-names-for-women-at-work.

———. "When People Assume You're Not in Charge Because You're a Woman." *Harvard Business Review*, December 22, 2021. https://hbr .org/2021/12/when-people-assume-youre-not-in-charge-because-youre -a-woman.

Diehl, Amy B., Leanne M. Dzubinski, and Amber L. Stephenson. "How Organizations Can Recognize—and End—Gendered Ageism." In *Overcoming Ageism*, 171–78. Women at Work Series. Harvard Business Review Press, 2024.

———. "Never Quite Right: Identity Factors Contributing to Bias and Discrimination Experienced by Women Leaders in the United States." *Human Resouce Development Quarterly* (2024): 1–20 (advance online publication).

———. "Women in Leadership Face Ageism at Every Age." *Harvard Business Review*, June 16, 2023. https://hbr.org/2023/06/women-in-leadership -face-ageism-at-every-age.

Diehl, Amy B., Amber L. Stephenson, Leanne M. Dzubinski, and David C. Wang. "Measuring the Invisible: Development and Multi-Industry Validation of the Gender Bias Scale for Women Leaders." *Human Resource Development Quarterly* 31, no. 3 (2020): 249–80.

Dingel, Molly, Marcia Nichols, Angie Mejia, and Kristin O'Siecki. "Service, Self-Care, and Sacrifice: A Qualitative Exploration of the Pandemic University as a Greedy Institution." *Advance* 2, no. 3 (2021): 1–10.

"Domestic Violence." National Coalition Against Domestic Violence, accessed April 3, 2025. https://assets.speakcdn.com/assets/2497/domestic _violence-2020080709350855.pdf?1596828650457,%20https://bjs.ojp.gov /female-murder-victims-and-victim-offender-relationship-2021.

Dorol-Beauroy-Eustache, Ophely, and Brian L. Mishara. "Systematic Review of Risk and Protective Factors for Suicidal and Self-Harm Behavior Among Children and Adolescents Involved with Cyberbullying." *Preventive Medicine* 152, no. 1 (2021).

Dyvik, Einar H. *Gender Poverty Gaps Worldwide in 2020 and 2021 (with a Forecast to 2030), by Gender.* Statista, accessed March 28, 2025. https:// www.statista.com/statistics/1219896/gender-poverty-gaps-worldwide-by -gender/.

Dzubinski, Leanne M. *Playing by the Rules: How Women Lead in Evangelical Mission Organizations.* American Society of Missiology Monograph Series 52. Pickwick, 2021.

———. "Portrayal vs. Practice: Contemporary Women's Contributions to Christian Mission." *Missiology: An International Review* 44, no. 1 (2016): 78–94.

———. "Taking on Power: Women Leaders in Evangelical Mission Organizations." *Missiology: An International Review* 44, no. 3 (2016): 281–95.

Dzubinski, Leanne M., and Amy B. Diehl. "The Problem of Gender Essentialism and Its Implications for Women in Leadership." *Journal of Leadership Studies* 12, no. 1 (2018): 56–61.

Dzubinski, Leanne M., M. Elizabeth Lewis Hall, and Richard L. Starcher. "The Stained-Glass Partition: Cross-Sex Collegial Relationships in Christian Academia." *Christian Higher Education* 20, no. 3 (2020): 184–208.

Dzubinski, Leanne M., and Anneke H. Stasson. *Women in the Mission of the Church: Their Opportunities and Obstacles Throughout Christian History*. Baker Academic, 2021.

Eagly, Alice H., and Steven J. Karau. "Role Congruity Theory of Prejudice Toward Female Leaders." *Psychological Review* 109, no. 3 (2002): 573–98.

Earls, Aaron, and Marissa Postell Sullivan. "Churchgoers and Leaders Find Value in Ministry to Women." Lifeway Research, October 17, 2023. https:// research.lifeway.com/2023/10/17/churchgoers-and-leaders-find-value-in -ministry-to-women/.

Eliason, Kristen Davis, Tamara Anderson, M. Elizabeth Lewis Hall, and Michele Willingham. "Where Gender and Religion Meet: Differentiating Gender Role Ideology and Religious Beliefs About Gender." *Journal of Psychology and Christianity* 36, no. 1 (2017): 3–15.

Ellison, Christopher G., and Jinwoo Lee. "Spiritual Struggles and Psychological Distress: Is There a Dark Side of Religion?" *Social Indicators Research* 98 (2010): 501–17.

Elsesser, Kim. *Sex and the Office: Women, Men, and the Sex Partition That's Dividing the Workplace*. Taylor Trade Publishing, 2015.

Elsesser, Kim, and Letitia Anne Peplau. "The Glass Partition: Obstacles to Cross-Sex Friendships at Work." *Human Relations* 59, no. 8 (2006): 1077–1100.

Elting, Liz. "More Women Lead Top Companies Than Ever, and It's Not Even Close to Enough." *Forbes*, June 15, 2024. https://www.forbes.com/sites /lizelting/2024/06/15/more-women-lead-top-companies-than-ever-and-its -not-even-close-to-enough/.

"Employment Differences of Men and Women Narrow with Educational Attainment." Bureau of Labor Statistics, July 28, 2023. https://www.bls .gov/opub/ted/2023/employment-differences-of-men-and-women-narrow -with-educational-attainment.htm.

Encyclopedia.com. "fictive kinship." Accessed November 17, 2023, https:// www.encyclopedia.com/reference/encyclopedias-almanacs-transcripts -and-maps/fictive-kinship.

"Facts and Figures: Ending Violence Against Women." UN Women, November 25, 2024. https://www.unwomen.org/en/articles/facts-and-figures /facts-and-figures-ending-violence-against-women.

Feenstra, Sanne, Janka I. Stoker, Joris Lammers, and Harry Garretsen. "Managerial Stereotypes Over Time: The Rise of Feminine Leadership." *Gender in Management: An International Journal* 38, no. 6 (2023): 770–83.

Folke, Olle, Johanna Rickne, Seiki Tanaka, and Yasuka Tateishi. "Sexual Harassment of Women Leaders." *Daedalus, the Journal of the American Academy of Arts & Sciences* 149, no. 1 (2020): 180–97.

Fox-Kirk, Wendy, Rita A. Gardiner, Hayley Finn, and Jennifer Chisholm. "Genderwashing: The Myth of Equality." *Human Resource Development International* 23, no. 5 (2020): 586–97.

Frame, Marsha Wiggins, and Constance L. Shehan. "Work and Well-Being in the Two-Person Career: Relocation Stress and Coping Among Clergy Husbands and Wives." *Family Relations*, no. 2 (1994): 196–205.

Francis-Wright, Isabelle, and Moustafa Ayad. "'Your Body, My Choice': Hate and Harassment Towards Women Spreads Online." Institute for Strategic Dialogue, November 8, 2024. https://www.isdglobal.org/digital _dispatches/your-body-my-choice-hate-and-harassment-towards-women -spreads-online.

Fricker, Miranda. *Epistemic Injustice: Power and the Ethics of Knowing.* Oxford University Press, 2007.

George, Erin, and Gretchen Livingston, "What You Need to Know About the Gender Wage Gap." Originally posted to *U.S. Department of Labor*, March 12, 2024. Now viewable at https://www.workplacefairness.org /what-you-need-to-know-about-the-gender-wage-gap/.

Gillard, Joe. "14 Colonial-Era Slang Terms to Work into Modern Conversation." Mental Floss, January 15, 2020. https://www.mentalfloss.com /article/612217/colonial-era-slang-terms.

Gillespie, Lane G. "Survey: 89% of American Workforce Prefer 4-Day Workweeks, Remote Work or Hybrid Work." Bankrate, August 23, 2023. https://www.bankrate.com/personal-finance/hybrid-remote-and-4-day -workweek-survey/.

Glick, Peter, Mariah Wilkerson, and Marshall Cuffe. "Masculine Identity, Ambivalent Sexism, and Attitudes Toward Gender Subtypes: Favoring Masculine Men and Feminine Women." *Social Psychology* 46, no. 4 (2015): 210–17.

Godsil, Rachel D., Linda R. Tropp, Phillip Atiba Goff, John A. Powell, and Jessica MacFarlane. *The Science of Equality.* Vol. 2, *The Effects of Gender Roles, Implicit Bias, and Stereotype Threat on the Lives of Women and Girls.* Perception Institute, 2016.

Graham, Ruth. "What the Latest Investigations into the Catholic Church Sex Abuse Mean." *New York Times*, June 2, 2023. https://www.nytimes.com /2023/06/02/us/catholic-church-sex-abuse-investigations.html.

Grant, Adam. "Are You Selfish or Just Busy? It Depends on Your Gender." *The Next Big Idea Club*, April 8, 2016. https://nextbigideaclub.com/magazine /adam-grant-selfish-just-busy-depends-gender/7361/.

"The Great Gloom: In 2023, Employees Are Unhappier Than Ever." Bamboo HR, 2023, https://www.bamboohr.com/resources/guides/employee-happiness-h1-2023.

Greenberg, Spencer, and Holly Muir. "Most of Us Combine Personality Traits from Different Genders." *Scientific American*, January 31, 2022. https://www.scientificamerican.com/article/most-of-us-combine-personality-traits-from-different-genders/.

Grudem, Wayne. "A Letter from Wayne Grudem." The Council on Biblical Manhood and Womanhood, September 28, 2020. https://cbmw.org/2020/09/28/a-letter-from-wayne-grudem/.

Hall, M. Elizabeth Lewis, Brad Christerson, and Shelly Cunningham. "Sanctified Sexism: Religious Beliefs and the Gender Harassment of Academic Women." *Psychology of Women Quarterly* 34, no. 2 (2010): 181–85.

Haslam, Nick, Louis Rothschild, and Donald Ernst. "Essentialist Beliefs About Social Categories." *British Journal of Social Psychology* 39, no. 1 (2000): 113–27.

Heath, Chip, and Dan Heath. *Switch: How to Change Things When Change Is Hard*. Currency, 2010.

Hinkley, Chesna, "4 Ways Complementarian Churches Can Be Better for Women." *CBE International*, December 13, 2017. https://www.cbeinternational.org/resource/4-ways-complementarian-churches-can-be-better-women/.

Hirschfield, Laura E., and Tiffany D. Joseph. "'We Need a Woman, We Need a Black Woman': Gender, Race, and Identity Taxation in the Academy." *Gender and Education* 24, no. 2 (2012): 213–27.

Homan, Patricia, and Amy Burdette. "When Religion Hurts: Structural Sexism and Health in Religious Congregations." *American Sociological Review* 86, no. 2 (2021): 234–55.

James, Carolyn Custis. *Half the Church: Recapturing God's Global Vision for Women*. Zondervan, 2011.

———. *When Life and Beliefs Collide: How Knowing God Makes a Difference*. Zondervan, 2001.

John, Ann, Alexander Charles Glendenning, Amanda Marchant, Paul Montgomery, Anne Steward, Sophie Wood, Keith Lloyd, and Keith Hawton. "Self-Harm, Suicidal Behaviours, and Cyberbullying in Children and Young People: Systematic Review." *Journal of Medical Internet Research* 20, no. 4 (2018): 1–15.

John Chrysostom. "Homily 34." In *Homilies on the Gospel of John*. https://www.newadvent.org/fathers/240134.htm.

Kahalon, Rotem, Nurit Shnabel, and Julia C. Becker. "'Don't Bother Your Pretty Little Head': Appearance Compliments Lead to Improved Mood but Impaired Cognitive Performance." *Psychology of Women Quarterly* 42, no. 2 (2018): 136–50.

"Karen Pence Is the Vice President's 'Prayer Warrior.'" *Washington Post*, March 28, 2017. https://www.washingtonpost.com/politics/karen-pence -is-the-vice-presidents-prayer-warrior-gut-check-and-shield/2017/03/28 /3d7a26ce-0a01-11e7-8884-96e6a6713f4b_story.html.

Katz, Daniel, Nathan Maccoby, Gerald Gurin, and Lucretia G. Floor. *Productivity, Supervision and Morale Among Raliroad Workers.* University of Michigan, 1951.

Katz, Daniel, Nathan Maccoby, and Nancy C. Morse. *Productivity, Supervision and Morale in an Office Situation.* University of Michigan, 1950.

Keener, Craig S. *The Gospel of Matthew: A Socio-Rhetorical Commentary.* Eerdmans, 2009.

Kerr, Glenn J. "Dynamic Equivalence and Its Daughters: Placing Bible Translation Theories in Their Historical Context." *Journal of Translation* 7, no. 1 (2011): 1–19.

King, Eden B., Michelle R. Hebl, Jennifer M. George, and Sharon F. Matusik. "Understanding Tokenism: Antecedents and Consequences of a Psychological Climate of Gender Inequity." *Journal of Management* 36, no. 2 (2010): 482–510.

Knox, John. *The First Blast of the Trumpet Against the Monstrous Regiment of Women.* London: 1558. https://www.gutenberg.org/files/9660 /9660-h/9660-h.htm.

Kobes Du Mez, Kristin. *Jesus and John Wayne: How White Evangelicals Corrupted a Faith and Fractured a Nation.* Liveright, 2020.

Kristof, Nicholas D., and Sheryl WuDunn. *Half the Sky: Turning Oppression into Opportunity for Women Worldwide.* Knopf, 2009.

Lee, Dorothy A. *The Ministry of Women in the New Testament: Reclaiming the Biblical Vision for Church Leadership.* Baker Academic, 2021.

Longman, Karen A., and Patricia S. Anderson. "Women in Leadership: The Future of Christian Higher Education." *Christian Higher Education* 15, nos. 1–2 (2016): 24–37.

Luther on Women: A Sourcebook. Translated by Susan C. Karant-Nunn and Merry E. Wiesner-Hanks. Cambridge University Press, 2003.

Maglaty, Jeanne. "When Did Girls Start Wearing Pink?" *Smithsonian Magazine*, April 7, 2011. https://www.smithsonianmag.com/arts-culture/when -did-girls-start-wearing-pink-1370097/.

Mathews, Alice P. *Gender Roles and the People of God: Rethinking What We Were Taught About Men and Women in the Church.* Zondervan, 2017.

———. *Preaching That Speaks to Women.* Baker Academic, 2003.

Mathews, Alice P., and M. Gay Hubbard. *Marriage Made in Eden: A Pre-Modern Perspective for a Post-Modern World*. Baker Books, 2004.

Matthews, Heather. *Confronting Sexism in the Church: How We Got Here and What We Can Do About It*. IVP, 2024.

McKnight, Scot. *Pastor Paul: Nurturing a Culture of Christoformity in the Church*. Theological Explorations for the Church Catholic. Brazos, 2019.

Melville, Doug. "Costco Doubled Down on DEI as a Business Case: What We Can All Learn." *Forbes*, December 30, 2024. https://www.forbes.com/sites/dougmelville/2024/12/30/costco-doubled-down-on-dei-as-a-business-case-what-we-can-all-learn/.

Merriam-Webster Dictionary. "Beg the question." Accessed April 1, 2025. https://www.merriam-webster.com/grammar/beg-the-question.

Merriam-Webster Dictionary. "Gay." Accessed March 20, 2025. https://www.merriam-webster.com/dictionary/gay.

Merriam-Webster Dictionary. "Mansplain." Accessed March 20, 2025. https://www.merriam-webster.com/dictionary/mansplain.

Meyer, Erin. *The Culture Map: Breaking Through the Invisible Boundaries of Global Business*. PublicAffairs, 2014.

Meyer, Marshall W. "Reviewed Work: *Greedy Institutions: Patterns of Undivided Commitment* by Lewis A. Coser." *American Journal of Sociology* 80, no. 6 (1975): 1495–96.

Mikołajczak, Małgorzata, and Janina Pietrzak. "Ambivalent Sexism and Religion: Connected Through Values." *Sex Roles* 70 (2014): 387–99.

Miller, Andrea L., and Eugene Borgida. "The Separate Spheres Model of Gendered Inequality." *PLoS ONE* 11, no. 1 (2016): 1–34.

Mirkus, Johannes. *Mirk's Festival: A Colletion of Homilies*. Edited by Theodor Erbe. Kegan Paul, 1905.

Mohr, Tara Sophia. "Why Women Don't Apply for Jobs Unless They're 100% Qualified." *Harvard Business Review*, August 25, 2014. https://hbr.org/2014/08/why-women-dont-apply-for-jobs-unless-theyre-100-qualified.

Moore, Beth. *All My Knotted-Up Life: A Memoir*. Tyndale, 2023.

Mounce, Bill. "Do Formal Equivalent Translations Reflect a Higher View of Plenary, Verbal Inspiration?" Evangelical Theological Association, Denver, CO, 2018. https://doxa.billmounce.com/Inspiration_and_Translation_Theory.pdf.

———. *What I Have Learned About Greek and Translation Since Joining the CBT*. Booklet, 2019. https://doxa.billmounce.com/What-I-Have-Learned-Bill-Mounce.pdf.

Mowczko, Marg, "'Brothers and Sisters' (Adelphoi) in Paul's Letters." *Exploring the Biblical Theology of Christian Egalitarianism* (blog), March 25, 2022. https://margmowczko.com/adelphoi-brothers-and-sisters/#_ftn1.

————. "Manhood and Masculinity in the ESV." *Exploring the Biblical Theology of Christian Egalitarianism* (blog), August 11, 2019. https://margmowczko.com/biblical-manhood-masculinity-esv/.

Murphy-Geiss, Gail. "Married to the Minister: The Status of the Clergy Spouse as Part of a Two-Person Single Career." *Journal of Family Issues* 32, no. 7 (2011): 932–55.

Nadworny, Elissa. "Liberty University Fined $14 Million for Federal Crime Reporting Violations." NPR, March 5, 2024. https://www.npr.org/2024/03/05/1236019397/liberty-university-clery-act-safety-crime.

Noland, Marcus, Tyler Moran, and Barbara Kotschwar. *Is Gender Diversity Profitable? Evidence from a Global Survey*. Peterson Institute for International Economics, 2016. https://www.piie.com/publications/working-papers/gender-diversity-profitable-evidence-global-survey.

Northouse, Peter G. *Leadership: Theory and Practice*. 8th ed. SAGE, 2019.

Papanek, Hanna. "Men, Women, and Work: Reflections on the Two-Person Career." *The American Journal of Sociology* 78, no. 4 (1973): 852–72.

Park, Andrea. "The Internet Is Loving This New Word for When a Man Repeats Your Idea and Gets Credit." Allure, September 25, 2017. https://www.allure.com/story/hepeat-twitter-reactions.

Payne, Philip Barton. *The Bible vs. Biblical Womanhood: How God's Word Consistently Affirms Gender Equality*. Zondervan, 2023.

Peterson, Abby, and Sara Uhnoo. "The Problem of Loyalty in Greedy Institutions." In *Psychology of Loyalty*, edited by L. B. Miller and W. C. Moore, 37–63. Nova Science Publishers, 2013.

Peterson, Miranda. "The Unfinished Fight for Equal Pay: How Women Fared in 2024." Institute for Women's Policy Research, December 19, 2024. https://iwpr.org/the-unfinished-fight-for-equal-pay-how-women-fared-in-2024/.

Pingleton, Susan K., Emily V. M. Jones, Tacey A. Rosolowski, and Mary K. Zimmerman. "Silent Bias: Challenges, Obstacles, and Strategies for Leadership Development in Academic Medicine—Lessons from Oral Histories of Women Professors at the University of Kansas." *Academic Medicine* 91, no. 8 (2016): 1151–57.

"Pope Admits Clerical Abuse of Nuns Including Sexual Slavery." *BBC*, February 6, 2019. https://www.bbc.com/news/world-europe-47134033.

Poverty Rates for Adults Ages 19–64 by Sex. Kaiser Family Foundation (2023). https://www.kff.org/other/state-indicator/adult-poverty-rate-by-sex/.

Prime, Jeanine L., Nancy M. Carter, and Theresa M. Welbourne. "Women 'Take Care,' Men 'Take Charge': Managers' Stereotypic Perceptions of Women and Men Leaders." *Psychologist-Manager Journal* 12, no. 1 (2009): 25–49.

Reeder, Caryn A. *The Samaritan Woman's Story: Reconsidering John 4 After #Churchtoo*. IVP, 2022.

Remery, Chantal, Richard J. Petts, Joop Schippers, and Mara A. Yerkes. "Gender and Employment: Recalibrating Women's Position in Work, Organizations, and Society in Times of COVID-19." *Gender, Work & Organization* 29, no. 6 (2022): 1927–34.

Reynolds, Amy, Janel Curry, and Neil Carlson. *Gender Dynamics in Evangelical Institutions: Women and Men Leading in Higher Education and the Non-Profit Sector*. Women in Leadership National Study. Gordon College, 2016. https://www.wheaton.edu/media/global-and-experiential-learning-gps/ntwk-inititv-gender-dev-christianity/FINAL_WILNSP1P2_December2016.pdf.

Ross, Cathy. "Separate Spheres or Shared Dominions?" *Transformation* 23, no. 4 (2006): 228–35.

Roys, Julie. "John MacArthur Tells Seminarians Not to Speak at Conferences with Women, Even Though He Has." *The Roys Report*, May 8, 2023. https://julieroys.com/john-macarthur-tells-seminarians-not-to-speak-at-conferences-with-women-even-though-he-has/.

Rudman, Laurie A., and Peter Glick. "Prescriptive Gender Stereotypes and Backlash Toward Agentic Women." *Journal of Social Issues* 57, no. 4 (2001): 743.

Rufkin, Bryan. "Why Do We Buy into the 'Cult' of Overwork?" Worklife, *BBC*, May 9, 2021. https://www.bbc.com/worklife/article/20210507-why-we-glorify-the-cult-of-burnout-and-overwork.

Sayers, Dorothy L. *Are Women Human? Penetrating, Sensible, and Witty Essays on the Role of Women in Society*. Eerdmans, 1971.

Schein, Virginia Ellen. "The Relationship Between Sex Role Stereotypes and Requisite Management Characteristics." *Journal of Applied Psychology* 57, no. 2 (1973): 95–100.

Schein, Virginia Ellen, Ruediger Mueller, Terri Lituchy, and Jiang Liu. "Think Manager—Think Male: A Global Phenomenon?" *Journal of Organizational Behavior* 17 (1996): 33–41.

Seerig, Kristen Hannah, Maximilian Haug, Alexander Maier, and Heiko Gewald. "The Healing Power of Words: Examining the Effect of Communication Styles on Appreciation Within the Hospital Setting." *Procedia Computer Science* 231 (2024): 305–10.

Segal, Mady Wechsler. "The Military and the Family as Greedy Institutions." *Armed Forces and Society* 13, no. 1 (1986): 9–38.

Sherman, Whitney H., Danna M. Beaty, Karen S. Crum, and April Peters. "Unwritten: Young Women Faculty in Educational Leadership." *Journal of Educational Administration* 48, no. 6 (2010): 741–54.

Solnit, Rebecca. "Men Explain Things to Me." *Guernica*, August 20, 2012. https://www.guernicamag.com/rebecca-solnit-men-explain-things-to-me/.

Southern Baptist Convention Executive Committee's Response to Sexual Abuse Allegations and an Audit of the Procedures and Actions of the Credentials Committee, The. Guidepost Solutions, May 15, 2022. https://www.documentcloud.org/documents/22028383-guidepost-investigation-of-the-southern-baptist-convention/.

State of Ministry to Women: Leaders Report. Lifeway Research, accessed March 28, 2025. https://research.lifeway.com/state-of-ministry-to-women/.

Stauffer, Dana Jalbert. "Aristotle's Account of the Subjection of Women." *The Journal of Politics* 70, no. 4 (2008): 929–41.

Stephenson, Amber L., Amy B. Diehl, Leanne M. Dzubinski, Marla McErlean, John Huppertz, and Mandeep Sidhu, eds. *An Exploration of Gender Bias Affecting Women in Medicine*. The Contributions of Health Care Management to Grand Health Care Challenges 20. Emerald, 2021.

Stewart, Heather. "'Why Didn't She Say Something Sooner?': Doubt, Denial, Silencing, and the Epistemic Harms of the #MeToo Movement." *South Central Review* 36, no. 2 (2019): 68–94.

Stogdill, Ralph M., and Alvin E. Coons, eds. *Leader Behavior: Its Description and Measurement*. Ohio Studies in Personnel 88. The Ohio State University, 1957.

Strader, Eiko, and Margaret Smith. "Some Parents Survive and Some Don't: The Army and the Family as 'Greedy Institutions.'" *Public Administration Review* 82, no. 3 (2022): 446–58.

"Survey: US Employees Prioritize Workplace Flexibility as a Key Component of Compensation." The Conference Board, November 7, 2023. https://www.conference-board.org/press/workplace-flexibility?tpcc=NL_Marketing.

Swartz, Lisa Weaver. "Gendered Gospel, Ungendered Mission: Identity Construction at Two Evangelical Seminaries." PhD diss., University of Notre Dame, 2017.

Tan, Valarie. "Women Hold Up Half the Sky, but Men Rule the Party." Mercator Institute for China Studies, July 3, 2021. https://merics.org/en/comment/women-hold-half-sky-men-rule-party.

Tannen, Deborah. "The Power of Talk: Who Gets Heard and Why." *Harvard Business Review* (September–October 1995): 138–48. https://hbr.org/1995 /09/the-power-of-talk-who-gets-heard-and-why.

Thomas Aquinas. Lecture 3 on John 20. In *Commentary on the Gospel of St. John.* Translated by James A. Weisheipl. Magi Books, 1998. https:// isidore.co/aquinas/english/SSJohn.htm.

Thornton, Brendan Jamal. "Victims of Illicit Desire: Pentecostal Men of God and the Specter of Sexual Temptation." *Anthropological Quarterly* 91, no. 1 (2018): 133–71.

Tracy, Sarah J., and Kendra Dyanne Rivera. "Endorsing Equity and Applauding Stay-at-Home Moms: How Male Voices on Work-Life Reveal Aversive Sexism and Flickers of Transformation." *Management Communication Quarterly* 24, no. 1 (2010): 3–43.

Trageser, Claire. "Stop Telling Women They're Amazing." *Elle*, February 24, 2021. https://www.elle.com/life-love/a35562291/stop-telling-women -theyre-amazing/.

Tremmel, Manuela, and Ingrid Wahl. "Gender Stereotypes in Leadership: Analysing the Content and Evaluation of Stereotypes About Typical, Male, and Female Leaders." *Frontiers in Psychology* 14 (2023): 1–17.

Tucker, Ruth A. *Black and White Bible, Black and Blue Wife: My Story of Finding Hope After Domestic Abuse.* Zondervan, 2016.

"20 Words That Once Meant Something Very Different." TED, June 18, 2014. https://ideas.ted.com/20-words-that-once-meant-something-very-different/.

Valiente, Celia. "Age and Feminist Activism: The Feminist Protest Within the Catholic Church in Franco's Spain." *Social Movement Studies* 14, no. 4 (2015): 473–92.

"Vatican Magazine Denounces Sexual Abuse of Nuns by Priests." *Irish Examiner*, February 1, 2019. https://www.irishexaminer.com/world/arid -30901659.html.

Webb, William J. *Slaves, Women and Homosexuals: Exploring the Hermeneutics of Cultural Analysis.* IVP Academic, 2001.

Weissenberg, Peter, and Michael J. Kavanagh. "The Independence of Initiating Structure and Consideration: A Review of the Evidence." *Personnel Psychology* 25, no. 1 (1972): 119–30.

"What's 'the Billy Graham Rule'?" Billy Graham Evangelistic Association, July 23, 2019. https://billygraham.org/story/the-modesto-manifesto -a-declaration-of-biblical-integrity/.

Wilkin, Jen. "Honor Thy Church Mothers—with Wages." *Christianity Today*, October 2023. https://www.christianitytoday.com/2023/09/wilkin -women-ministry-leaders-church-staff-wages-lifeway/.

Woodruff, Kelsey Hanson. "A Calculated Attack on Clergy Abuse: Challenging Patriarchal Power at Willow Creek Community Church." *Theology and Sexuality* 30, no. 1 (2024): 32–49.

Wright, Mary C., Nandini Assar, Edward L. Kain, Laura Kramer, Carla B. Howery, Kathleen McKinney, Becky Glass, and Maxine Atkinson. "Greedy Institutions: The Importance of Institutional Context for Teaching in Higher Education." *Teaching Sociology* 32, no. 2 (2004): 144–59.

Zhang, Tingting, and Chloe Rodrigue. "What If Moms Quiet Quit? The Role of Maternity Leave Policy in Working Mothers' Quiet Quitting Behaviors." *Merits* 3, no. 1 (2023): 186–205.

Index

Abigail, 63–64, 118
abuse, power and, 107–12, 113
Acker, Joan, 47, 50
address, forms of
 "brother" and "sister," 15
 "ladies," 16
 omission of titles, 74, 77–78, 83,
  93–94
 pet names and diminutives, 73, 74,
  76–77, 78, 83, 93
adelphos, adelphoi, 10–11, 29n19
ageism, 74
agentic qualities
 associated with men, 99–102,
  104–5
 vs. communal qualities, 102–3
 of leaders, 100–101, 121–22
 of women, 102, 105–6, 118–19
allies, 43–44, 117–19, 122–23,
 133–34
ambivalence. *See* women, ambivalence toward
Argyris, Chris, 112
Aristotle, 36, 75
Asbury Theological Seminary, 52n17

attitudes toward women
 ambivalence communicated by, 74,
  75, 81–85
 changing, 15, 131–35
 in leadership, 102–3, 106
 throughout history, xxi, 35–36, 75,
  85, 86
 See also under women
attrition rates, 7

backlash, 35, 79
Barr, Beth Allison, 39, 82–83
Barrero, Jose, 68
Barrows, Cliff, 2n2
Bauman, Andrew, 111
behavior
 ambivalence communicated by,
  74–75, 76–83
 changing, 15, 131–35
benevolent sexism, 75, 83–84, 95
bias, cultural, 61–62, 126–27, 128–29
Bible, women in, 62–64, 87–93, 117–19
Bible translation
 approaches to, 27–29, 38, 42–43
 cultural assumptions in, 61–62

Index